SWARMING &

The Future of Conflict

John Arquilla   David Ronfeldt

Office of the Secretary of Defense

RAND

National Defense Research Institute

This documented briefing continues the elaboration of our ideas about how the information revolution is affecting the whole spectrum of conflict. Our notion of cyberwar (1993) focused on the military domain, while our study on netwar (1996) examined irregular modes of conflict, including terror, crime, and militant social activism. Here we advance the idea that swarming may emerge as a definitive doctrine that will encompass and enliven both cyberwar and netwar. This doctrinal proposal relates to our efforts to flesh out a four-part vision of how to prepare for information-age conflict (see Arquilla and Ronfeldt, 1997, Ch. 19).

We have argued, first of all, for adopting a broad concept of "information"—so that it is defined as something that refers not only to communications media and the messages transmitted, but also to the increasingly material "information content" of all things, including weapons and other sorts of systems. The next part of our vision focused on the organizational dimension, emphasizing that the information revolution empowers the network form—undermining most hierarchies. Moving on to the third part, we then exposited our ideas about developing an American grand strategy based on "guarded openness"—a principle that, for example, encourages reaching out widely with ideas about freedom and progress, while still being circumspect about diffusion of advanced information processes and technologies.

In this document, we complete our four-part vision by articulating a doctrine we call "swarming," and which we believe may eventually apply across the entire spectrum of conflict—from low to high intensity, and from civic-oriented actions to military combat operations on land, at sea, and in the air.

Primarily of interest to U.S. policymakers and strategists, this documented briefing will also interest those in academia and research institutes concerned with how the information revolution is altering the nature of conflict.

This study was prepared for a project on "Swarming and Information Operations." The project was sponsored by the Office of the Assistant Secretary of Defense (Command, Control, Communications and Intelligence), OASD/C3I, and was conducted within the International Security and Defense Policy Center of RAND's National Defense Research

Institute (NDRI). NDRI is a federally funded research and development center sponsored by the Office of the Secretary of Defense, the Joint Staff, the unified commands, and the defense agencies.

Readers should also see a companion study by Sean Edwards, *Swarming on the Battlefield: Past, Present, and Future* (RAND, 2000). It provides additional historical background and analysis.

Comments are invited. We are available via email, arquilla@rand.org and ronfeldt@rand.org.

CONTENTS

Swarming is seemingly amorphous, but it is a deliberately structured, coordinated, strategic way to strike from all directions, by means of a sustainable pulsing of force and/or fire, close-in as well as from stand-off positions. It will work best—perhaps it will only work—if it is designed mainly around the deployment of myriad, small, dispersed, networked maneuver units (what we call "pods" organized in "clusters"). Developing a swarming force implies, among other things, radical changes in current military organizational structures. From command and control of line units to logistics, profound shifts will have to occur to nurture this new "way of war." Our study examines the benefits—and also the costs and risks—of engaging in such serious doctrinal change.

Examples of swarming can be found throughout history, but it is only now able to emerge as a doctrine in its own right. That is largely because swarming depends on a devolution of power to small units and a capacity to interconnect those units that has only recently become feasible, due to the information revolution.

Briefly, we advance the idea that swarming—engaging an adversary from all directions simultaneously, either with fire or in force—is one of four types of doctrine that have long been around. The other forms are the chaotic melee, brute-force massing, and nimble maneuver. Each form has had a different information requirement—melees requiring the least, maneuvers needing more than massing, and swarming depending completely on robust, rapid communications. While all the forms have been around throughout history, melees and massing appear to have been dominant at the tactical level primarily in pre-industrial times. Such paragons of maneuver as Alexander the Great and Genghis Khan are overshadowed by a long procession of mass-oriented militaries—a point borne out by the brief eminence of the empires they created.

Over the past two centuries, however, mass and maneuver have followed a much more interactive pattern, featuring the dominance of the former, at times (e.g., as in World War I)—but also of the latter (e.g., in World War II). We argue that the rise of advanced information operations will bring swarming to the fore, establishing a new pattern in conflict.

This study derives insights from examples of swarming in nature and in history. Both areas are replete with instances of omnidirectional yet well-timed assaults. From ants and bees and wolf packs, to ancient Parthians and medieval Mongols, swarming in force, or of fire, has often proven a very effective way of fighting.

Some societies have already had a great deal of exposure to and practical experience with swarming. The British, for example, pioneered a kind of swarming in the naval doctrine they followed in their fight against the Spanish Armada in 1588—in this case a swarming of fire that relentlessly harried the invasion fleet and hastened it toward its destruction. Later on, in the 18th century, the British Army would have to deal with the swarming fire of American rebels—with which it never fully coped. However, another century later, in the Zulu War of 1879, the British Army would defeat a sophisticated swarming-in-force doctrine—after but one early reverse. Then, during World War II, the British would use defensive swarming in force to win the Battle of Britain and defeated the swarming U-boat wolfpack doctrine in a protracted Battle of the Atlantic. Information operations played crucial roles in the outcomes of both campaigns.

The historical insight that information flows (or their disruption) provide a key, both to understanding and practicing swarming, should encourage U.S. military leaders to view information operations as a central element in the development of future military doctrine. Already, a number of interesting initiatives are under way—from the Army's Experimental Force to the Navy's "network-centric warfare" notions. The Marines and the Air Force are also well represented when it comes to thinking about future operations. Yet, our survey of recent developments found that none of the ongoing experiments has articulated an explicit doctrine that will help prepare the U.S. military for conflict in the coming decades.

Swarming could become the catalyst for the creation of a newly energized military doctrine: "BattleSwarm." One requirement—well-informed, deadly small units—is already coming into being. But getting them properly networked and getting a new doctrine to take hold will not be an easy process, given the continued popularity and apparent utility of the current AirLand Battle doctrine. Swarming implies radical new changes in current military organization—including the elimination of many formations above the company level. Swarming, and the nonlinear battlespace that it envisions, will also require the development of a new logistical paradigm. The current one is over three hundred years old and, although it has often worked well, it is mass-oriented—and thus unsuited to swarming operations.

Finally, nimble information operations (IO)—especially the part of IO that has to do with managing one's own information flows—will be necessary if swarming is to take hold. This puts a premium on robust communications capable of resisting very determined disruptive action. This may be achieved—but it will only be sustained if a new "turn of mind" that is cognizant of the overall value of IO in military affairs is cultivated.

We are thankful for thoughtful, encouraging comments provided by RAND colleagues Sean Edwards, Jeff Isaacson, and Michele Zanini in the course of preparing this study. We are also indebted to Dick O'Neill and many other members of the Highlands Forum for the various discussions about swarming that we have had with them over the past several years. Elsewhere, Bob Scott and Alvin Toffler both prodded us to refine our thinking on this topic. Bevin Alexander and RAND colleague Martin Libicki wrote insightful reviews that directed us to clarify and sharpen our ideas. Finally, we are grateful for the support and useful guidance provided to us by the Assistant Secretary of Defense (C3I), Art Money; his Principal Deputy, Lin Wells; Colonel Robert Blunden, USAF, retired; and Lieutenant Colonel Robert Walter, USA.

Swarming and the Future of Conflict

John Arquilla and David Ronfeldt

Theorists and practitioners around the world, allies as well as adversaries, are well into a decade of wondering how the information age may reshape the nature of conflict. The Gulf War continues to provide the most marvelous image of the U.S. military mounting high-tech, fast-moving, coordinated strikes, applying its innovative AirLand Battle doctrine to defeat an enemy's regular military formations. Yet, this war may mark the end of an era more than the start of a new one for U.S. doctrine and strategy in the information age. Other models—far more irregular in nature—are also on the rise.

The wars in Somalia and Kosovo have shown that ethnonationalist paramilitary bands, organized in small, dispersed units, can wreak havoc and confound U.S. and allied operations, at least for awhile—in Somalia despite a mobile U.S. ground presence, and in Kosovo despite U.S. air superiority. In Chechnya, the Russian military continues to face even more serious opposition from battle-minded clans. As this level of warfare has been evolving, all U.S. services have been experimenting, some quite successfully, with how to design and employ new kinds of light, mobile, technologically advanced forces for potential major regional contingencies in various theaters—but doctrines are still lacking to make these new approaches entirely effective.

In the middle of the conflict spectrum where military affairs fade into police matters, new generations of terrorists and criminals, both at home and abroad, are also pursuing innovations as a result of the information revolution. They are organizing into loose, transnational networks that allow for increased coordination and cooperation among dispersed groups and individuals who are able to stay securely separated in case any one is caught and incriminated. For example, some leaders of the sprawling radical right in the United States subscribe to a doctrine of "leaderless resistance" that can motivate "lone wolves" to commit violent acts entirely on their own account.

At the social end of the conflict spectrum, the Zapatista movement in Mexico, which fused the Zapatista National Liberation Army (EZLN) with a transnational network of sympathetic nongovernmental organizations (NGOs), kept the Mexican government and army on the defensive for several years by means of aggressive but peaceful information operations. Meanwhile, the International Campaign to Ban Landmines (ICBL) grew into an effective global political movement—winning the Nobel Peace Prize—by using the Internet to assemble and coordinate a complex network of supportive NGOs and governments. Most recently, massive protest demonstrations by activists who swarmed into Seattle, following months of organization across the Internet, shut down the opening day of a major meeting of the World Trade Organization—and disrupted and overshadowed the full proceedings.

Furthermore, all across the conflict spectrum, computer hackers are on the move, with their stealthy, disruptive techniques. Serb hackers have defaced NATO web sites. Pro-Zapatista hackers have used an instrument called FloodNet to try to take down Mexican government and U.S. corporate web sites. Chinese and Taiwanese hackers have sparred with each other over security matters. Unknown hackers, using Russian servers, have broken into sensitive U.S. military computer systems.

These are just a handful from a steady stream of cases, spanning the conflict spectrum, that are indicating how people may prefer to fight as the information age deepens. Each case has its own unique features, and a somewhat different mixture of pre- and post-modern characteristics. But collectively they speak to the growing power of small units, groups, and individuals who are able to connect and act conjointly by adopting network forms of organization and related doctrines and strategies and technologies. More than that, these cases speak to the rise of "swarming" as a mode of conflict.

For American political and military leaders, understanding the rise of swarming should lead to reappraisals of both our mass-oriented, industrial-age way of war, and of the statist focus of our diplomacy. In the future, we shall have to learn to fight nimbly against an array of armed adversaries who will likely do all they can to avoid facing us head-on in battle. Indeed, in the military arena, swarming has the potential to become a new doctrine (we call it "BattleSwarm") that will reshape the future of conflict as surely as the rise of blitzkrieg altered the face of modern war—from the Battle of France in 1940, to

Operation Desert Storm half a century later. Last, we shall also find, in day-to-day diplomacy, that networked nonstate actors, particularly those associated with a nascent global civil society, may raise political and social challenges and opportunities that differ radically from those we have traditionally confronted, or desired.

For the rest of the world, swarming will probably seem like a double-edged sword. Sometimes it may be viewed in a threatening light, as yet another concept emanating from the Americans, seeming to increase their power more than ever. But swarming may also be welcomed by many actors around the world as a way to reshape global competition and assemble social forces to overturn the existing order of world power led by the United States.

Insights From *In Athena's Camp*

- **Organizational imperative: Adopt network forms**
  - **New technologies devolve power, mobility to small forces, imperil large traditional formations**
  - **Whoever masters network form gains advantages**
- **Doctrinal imperative: Build on concept of swarming**
  - **Behavior that is most effective for networks of small, dispersed, mobile units that have topsight**
  - **Swarming emerging across spectrum of conflict**

✔ **Organization and doctrine as important as technology**

How people fight is a function of more than just technology. Technology matters (see Van Creveld, 1989). But a simple effort to incorporate a radically new technology into an established concept is often a recipe for trouble. Thus the *mitrailleuse,* an early machine gun that worked well, was available to the French Army in 1870 and would have decimated the Prussians in the field. But because it came on a gun carriage, it was kept back with the artillery—where it did little good. A modern example, one that reflects the implications of the information revolution, concerns the U.S. Army's "Force XXI." It is highly digitized—but this effort at wiring a whole force creates a cascade of incoming information that has at times greatly debilitated the command and control of the force in warfighting experiments because organizational redesigns have not accompanied the technological advances.

Our previous studies—notably *In Athena's Camp* (Arquilla and Ronfeldt, 1997)—have emphasized that the information revolution is altering the ways people fight across the spectrum of conflict. It is doing so mainly by improving the power and performance of small units, and by favoring the rise of network forms of organization, doctrine, and strategy, while making life difficult for large, traditional hierarchical forms. Technology matters, yes, but so does the form of organization that is adopted or developed to embrace it. A proper organizational form can empower the technology, as, for example, the creation of the panzer division allowed blitzkrieg to flourish.

Today, the key form of organization on the rise is the network, especially the all-channel network. The new information technologies render an ability to connect and coordinate the actions of widely distributed "nodes" in almost unprecedented ways. Whoever masters this form will accrue advantages of a substantial nature. Yet, networking alone is not enough; just organizing into a network is no guarantee of success. There must also be principles and practices—a doctrine—to guide what a networked force should do and how it should behave.

In *In Athena's Camp*, we speculated that swarming is already emerging as an appropriate doctrine for networked forces to wage information-age conflict. This nascent doctrine derives from the fact that robust connectivity allows for the creation of a multitude of small units of maneuver, networked in such a fashion that, although they might be widely distributed, they can still come together, at will and repeatedly, to deal resounding blows to their adversaries. This study builds on these earlier findings by inquiring at length into why and how swarming might be emerging as a preferred mode of conflict for small, dispersed, internetted units. In our view, swarming will likely be the future of conflict.

Our hypothesis about swarming is that the technical tools to support it already exist (e.g., unmanned aerial vehicles, precision-guided munitions and very advanced communications). So, moving toward swarming is going to be more a function of cultivating an appropriate turn of mind and a supple, networked military form of organization than it will be a search for new technologies. This notion seems already to be borne out by the Marine Corps' various experiments with its new operational concepts (Sea Dragon)—which use existing technology and emphasize networks.

This study focuses mainly on military swarming. Its effectiveness could prove high at all levels of military conflict, from major theater wars to small-scale contingencies. Against a conventional adversary on a traditional battlefield, the swarming of directed fires should have devastating effects. Against an elusive opponent trying to fight in an irregular fashion, the coordinated swarming of networked forces should enable them to defeat the enemy in detail. However, it should be noted that even a networked swarm force will have a hard time dealing with guerrilla forces enjoying the support of a populace that can sustain, hide, and nurture them.

We also attend, though secondarily, to swarming by nonmilitary actors that rely on violence, such as terrorist, criminal, and fanatical groups, and to swarming by social actors, such as civil-society NGOs whose practices are fundamentally peaceful.[1] In all these

---

[1]Other kinds of swarming, such as may be found among media and market actors, receive scant attention in this study but are certainly worthy of study since they exhibit related dynamics.

areas, the United States may often be on the receiving end of swarming behavior; so including them in our analysis should prove instructive for learning how to counter and cope with hostile military swarms.

The study concludes by proposing that development of a new "BattleSwarm" doctrine could prove fruitful for the U.S. military, perhaps more so than the further refinement of the AirLand Battle doctrine. We envision the development of new kinds of small military units called "pods" that can operate in "clusters." These units should be dispersed to mitigate the risk posed by hostile fire. Yet, they would feature great mobility, modest logistical requirements, and "topsight" (i.e., they will know much of what's going on in the overall campaign—as will their top commander). Possessing both mobility and situational knowledge, they will be able to strike, swarming from all directions, either with fire or in force.

A broader notion is also implied by this study: By learning to work with both the military and nonmilitary aspects of swarming—through innovative thinking about how best to blend all the military, diplomatic, and social dynamics of this phenomenon—a new paradigm may be built, at the highest level, for "strategic swarming."[2]

---

[2]We are grateful to Colonel Robert Blunden (USAF, retired) for suggesting this phrase.

Information and the Evolution of Military Organization and Doctrine

- **Four paradigms have emerged across the ages:**
  - **1. the melee**
  - **2. massing**
  - **3. maneuver**
  - **4. swarming**

- **Each builds on and incorporates what went before**

- **Each reflects information, communication advances**
  - **In information-processing capabilities**
  - **In embedded "structural information"**

- **Swarming enabled by latest information revolution**

As we observe in earlier writings (Arquilla and Ronfeldt, 1997, 1998a), the history of military organization and doctrine is largely a history of the progressive development of four fundamental forms of engagement: the melee, massing, maneuver, and swarming. Briefly, warfare has evolved from chaotic melees in which every man fought on his own, to the design of massed but often rigidly shaped formations, and then to the adoption of maneuver. Swarming appears at times in this history, but its major advances as a doctrine will occur in the coming years.

Organizations evolve according to the information that can be embedded in and processed by them. The skillful conduct of all modes of conflict requires information— both embedded structural information, so that people know (and are trained to know) what to do and why in an organized manner, and information-processing systems, so they can spot attacks and targets, identify friend from foe, and coordinate operations. Each stage in the progression noted above represents a higher level of organization, and each depends on the existence of ever more advanced information structuring and processing systems. Stated another way, each stage is associated with a progression in the quantity and quality of information, from both structural and processing viewpoints.[3]

When there was little reason to train as a body, little ability to communicate during battle with one's own forces, and only notional understandings of the opponent's intentions, the free-for-all melee dominated. As means of signaling emerged (e.g., semaphores) and weaponry was introduced that benefited from coordinated fire (e.g., muskets), more controlled formations came into being (usually linear in nature). Further advances in organization and technology led to ever more supple maneuver capabilities, with mobile columns to some extent replacing linear formations (Van Creveld, 1989; Keegan, 1993). This progression in organization and doctrine—from the melee, to massing, to maneuver, and onward to swarming—appears in all the realms of war: on land, at sea, and in the air. While this progression applies mainly to the history of military warfare, it has counterparts in the history of social movements as well.[4]

The melee, a chaotic, undirected clash of arms at close quarters, is the earliest of the four to have appeared, and the least demanding in terms of organization and information. Massing probably began to emerge somewhere in our distant past, as it was noticed that, by remaining nearby one's fellows, advantages were to be had. One might derive some protection, therefore, from being in a mass, as well as improve the overall striking power of the army. As massed formations took deliberate shape, battle became more of a bloody shoving match; but at least it featured somewhat cohesive sides.

These early "ways of war" had to await advances in both organization and information flows before maneuver could emerge. But with the redesign of a generic armed force into several smaller units, each commanded by a field grade leader, the possibility of more complex operations arose. Some of the force could defend while the rest attacked, for example, enabling the rise of the essence of maneuver—which has always aimed at striking one small part of an enemy force with a larger mass of one's own, crushing it in detail. The emergence of writing and literacy facilitated the rise of elaborate mass and maneuver operations. Writing made possible the conveyance of orders, both before and during battle, and made sense of the notion of creating many smaller units of maneuver beyond the immediate command of the leader. Later, along with mechanization, the spread of the telegraph and the radio fostered the development of more advanced maneuver doctrines.

To these three traditional approaches to battle, we add a fourth: swarming. By this we mean the systematic pulsing of force and/or fire by dispersed, internetted units, so as to strike the adversary from all directions simultaneously. This does not necessitate sur-

---

[3]The distinction between information structuring and information processing—and the importance of emphasizing the structuring as well as the processing roles of information—is discussed in Arquilla and Ronfeldt, 1997, 1998b.

[4]This four-part analysis of the evolution of military organization and doctrine has its origins in the four-part framework about the organizational forms (tribes, institutions, markets, and networks) that lie behind long-range social evolution (see Ronfeldt, 1996).

rounding the enemy, though swarming may include encirclement in some cases. Rather, emphasis is placed on forces or fires that can strike at will—wherever they will. Historically, there have been a few instances of this approach to battle. For example, swarming can be glimpsed in some ancient mounted armies (e.g., Parthians, Scythians, even the imperial Byzantine cavalry) that gave fits to phalanxes, legions, and other conventional military formations (see Edwards, 2000, for a historical overview). Better examples appear in the Mongol approach to war, in Mao Zedong's concept of "Peoples War," and in the Battle of Britain. But swarming could not come into its own as a major way of war, because its organizational and informational requirements are huge. Swarming has had to wait for the current information and communications revolution to unfold as robustly as did the earlier forms of fighting.

Each of the four forms incorporates and builds upon what came before. Aspects of the melee remain in present-day close-in, hand-to-hand combat. And the role of mass lives on in more sophisticated, maneuver-oriented forms of battle (e.g., AirLand Battle); but it is much transformed. Massing is still a crucial element in maneuver—but it is massing at the "decisive point," as Jomini, the great interpreter of Napoleonic strategy ([1838] 1992) called it, that counts most of all. Similarly, the melee will likely still have a role with the advent of swarming—but this nonlinear, very often close-in approach to fighting will be organized rather than chaotic. The information structuring (the "embedding" of all manner of information in the new military organizational forms) and processing done to prepare for and then to conduct battles will allow for controllable swarm tactics to emerge that may make an adversary think he is being overwhelmed in melee. But there will be far more structure to the attack than he may be able to discern. At least this is the ideal of the swarming concept—an ideal heavily reliant upon robust information flows and the development of junior-level officers who can think in high-level ways. Needless to say, these challenges for communications and command are substantial; and they suggest that a swarming force, when it fights close in, may often skitter along on the chaotic edge of an uncontrolled melee.

Since the newest approach to war may contain within it the oldest, theorists and practitioners should remain alert to the persistence of *all four* forms. Mass and maneuver have not gone away and may persist even in a conflict spectrum that may one day be dominated by swarming. Indeed, one need only look at the maneuvers-gone-awry of Task Force Ranger in Somalia in 1993 (see Bowden, 1999) to observe that some adversaries may actually cultivate opportunities to engage in modern-day melees where they detect vulnerabilities in a major power's operational stance.

The Melee—Earliest Form of Organization (and Doctrine)

- **Basic characteristics**
  - **Linear face-offs, easily dissolved formations**
  - **Command, control nearly impossible during battle**
- **Enabling technologies: eyes, ears; waving, shouting**
- **Historical cases**
  - **Land: Ancient Persian, Asiatic armies, feudal warfare**
  - **Sea: Naval battles until Drake (16th century)**
  - **Air: Dogfights of World War I**
  - **Social: Tribal conflicts; Paris during French Revolution**

The melee emerged out of necessity. Quite simply, for a long time there was virtually no way to maintain command or control of an armed force that had neither much organization nor smooth information flows. This was, basically, the primeval state of war, and it persisted for many millennia (Turney-High, 1949). Attempts to line up or face off against the enemy were sometimes made; but no battle plan or formation could persist well beyond the first clashing of arms. The only communications available were shouts and waving for the transmission of messages, and eyes and ears for reception. Battles often dissolved into bunching and rushing and flailing, man to man, rather like what may still be seen today in a chaotic bar, street, or gang fight.

This chaotic form of war persisted into the historical era and dominated even among the first of the Asiatic empires of the Sumerians, Akkadians, as well as others. In Europe, during the dark feudal age after the fall of Rome, a period of technical stagnation and social dissolution, European warfare once again reverted to the melee—seemingly wiping out the gains in massing and maneuvering that constituted hard-won progress in military affairs made over many centuries, including by the Greeks and the Romans.

The melee is found in all forms of early conflict. On land, the melee was a prominent form of fighting among countless primitive tribes and among the earliest empires. It may have been best exemplified, though, by the German resistance to Roman invasion in the early common era (9–18 A.D.). Led by Arminius, the Germans took good advantage of their heavily forested terrain to force the Romans into breaking their legionary formations, which resulted in fighting that consisted of a wild, extended series of small hand-to-hand combats. The Romans suffered a terrible loss at the outset of this struggle, in the Teutoberg Forest. But even after they rebounded, under the skillful Germanicus, winning at Idistaviso, the ferocity of the Germans convinced the Empire to expand no further than the Rhine and the Danube (Delbrueck, [1921] 1990, pp. 97–109, 149–159). After the fall of Rome in the fifth century, the next thousand years of European land warfare would be characterized generally by melees. Only the rise of the longbow would be able to break the spell of this form of warfare.

At sea a similar pattern was followed, over roughly the same period, with troop-laden, oar-powered galleys always aiming at getting close enough to the enemy to be able to fight hand-to-hand melees like those on land. This pattern persisted even into the 16th century, as the Christian and Turkish fleets that fought at Lepanto in 1571 (see Figure 1) were closely and hotly engaged for the better part of a day. Even the widespread presence of firearms and naval artillery did not work against the melee. However, in 1588, the embryonic British Royal Navy would hold off the Spanish Armada with firepower alone, marking the end of the era of naval melees (see Rodgers, 1940; Padfield, 1988).

Although air warfare did not emerge until the 20th century, it too followed the pattern of being dominated by the melee in its infancy. In this case, the air battles were called "dog-fights," a term that clearly evokes the chaotic nature of this mode of conflict. World War I in the air was dominated by the melee, since there was no way, beyond wing-waggling and hand signals, to control air forces during battle. Further, there were no electronic means of detecting enemy air movements under way, leading to a large number of unplanned "meeting engagements" (see Mitchell, [1928] 1960; Overy, 1997). Although this would change in World War II—and even more in subsequent wars—the aerial melee has never entirely disappeared; and dogfighting skills remain highly valued even in the missile age.

Finally, at the level of social conflict, the melee has been evident from very early times. A good example is the social chaos that came with "mobocracy" as found in Plato's recounting of Athenian life and political processes in the wake of the Peloponnesian War (ended in 404 B.C.), which culminated in the call for Socrates' execution for "impiety" (see Stone, 1989). After the fall of Greece (which coincided closely with the death of Socrates), democracy seldom took hold, flaring up decisively only in the American and French Revolutions of the late 18th century. And in both—but especially the French case—mob-driven melees played important roles in popular conflicts with authorities.[5] Invention of the telegraph helped move social activism away from uncoordinated mob melees and toward something more strategic and purposive—as seen in the social revolutions of 1848 in Europe.

---

[5]This is a central theme of Thomas Carlyle's ([1837] 1955) classic study of the French Revolution.

The Battle of Lepanto, 7 October 1571, ©National Maritime Museum, London.

Figure 1—The Melee at Lepanto

Next Development: Massing

- **Basic characteristics**
  - **Stacked, geometric formations for set-piece battles, with a front, a rear, and "waves"**
  - **Doctrines for maintaining hierarchy, shape, thrust**
- **Enabling technologies: writing; signaling systems; drilling routines—extending "reach" and discipline**
- **Historical cases**
  - **Land: Alexander's Greek phalanxes vs. Persian hordes**
  - **Sea: Rigid British, Dutch lines of battle (17th century)**
  - **Air: Bomber formations in WWII, also Vietnam**
  - **Social: Urban riots throughout Europe in 1848**

As the ability to command and control ever-larger forces improved, it grew incumbent upon military leaders to achieve advantages in mass over their adversaries. Strategy and tactics came to focus upon the various means by which the most force could be brought together on the battlefield, to provide maximum shock and firepower. This new emphasis encouraged the growth of well-articulated formations, featuring stacking and a geometric approach to set-piece battles with clearly defined fronts and rear areas. A premium was placed on the ability to keep some forces nearby, but not hotly engaged, so as to make them available for "wave" attacks, and as a reserve of mass to be employed at the decisive point and time. Military doctrine became very hierarchically oriented in pursuit of mass, because the maintenance of formation was crucially important to the continuing ability to apply mass in battle.

Written orders provided the first opportunity for armies to undertake field operations beyond the voice command of the general. But instructions alone could not guide a force engaged in a fluid, developing battle. For this, it grew necessary to develop signaling systems that would provide "real-time" aids for junior commanders. Thus, from mirrors, flags, and semaphores to the modern radio, signaling systems have played a vital role in the ability to apply mass on the battlefield. A further refinement favoring massing was the development of drilling routines, which both socialized the combat forces themselves and provided the tactical means for getting them to the battle and ensuring that their impact would have maximum effect. In essence, the communications technologies were ever extending the "reach" of forces, and drilling routines were enhancing their discipline, ensuring that troops would enter battle at the peak of their combat potential (McNeill, 1982, pp. 125–132).

The sixteen-deep ranks of the Greek phalanx were the ultimate expression of mass in the ancient world; and this formation gave Alexander the Great's forces a massed "punch" that simply could not be equaled. His ability to apply this mass in battle, and to integrate its use with his mounted maneuver forces, gave him an advantage that was unequaled in his era. In particular, his victory over the Persian empire demonstrated that massing and maneuvering toward the "decisive point" in battle could allow an overall smaller force to defeat a much larger enemy in detail (see Fuller, 1960, pp. 147–199). The Persians had far greater numbers of troops, but their loose, undisciplined formations and inability to maintain command and control ensured that Alexander's much smaller force would retain a decisive advantage.[6]

The paradigm provided by Alexander would serve well when military affairs were revived during the Renaissance and the Enlightenment; and even as late as the Thirty Years' War (1618–1648), his techniques of mass, drill, and discipline would remain decisive. Indeed, the zenith of mass-oriented battle may have been reached in the campaigns of the brilliant Swedish general Gustavus Adolphus, whose greatest victory, Breitenfeld (see Figure 2), was a testament to the power of localized, concentrated mass. Of equal importance to Gustavus, though, was the discipline and drill of his forces, enabling him to blend skillfully the strengths of muskets (fire) and pikes (shock) into a battle-winning combined arms approach to warfare (Wedgwood, 1938; Liddell Hart, 1927; Roberts, 1967).

At sea, the Royal Navy's defeat of the Armada with massed firepower soon led to an emphasis on strict adherence to formations that kept ships close enough together to bring their combined firepower down on an opposing force in as well-timed a manner as possible. This led to the development of the "line of battle" and the "ship of the line." Because of the emphasis on mass, naval doctrine (and formations) became very rigid. The exemplars of this approach to war at sea were the British and Dutch, who fought three bitter naval wars against each other during the 17th century. Each side enjoyed often brilliant leadership from their admirals: the Dutch from De Ruyter and Tromp, the British from Monck. What all three had in common was their devotion to the principle of mass and their ability to instill both the discipline and the drill necessary to fight in very compact, controlled formations for hours, sometimes days, on end (see Mahan, 1890; Barzun, 1944; and Marcus, 1961). This devotion to mass, seemingly for its own sake, would survive even the transition from sail to steam, and to long-range guns, and would characterize the Anglo-German engagement at Jutland in 1916 (see Bennett, 1964).

---

[6]Of course, the long spears of the heavy Greek infantry were crucial to success. But they were only effective to the extent to which formations, instilled by drill, could be kept, or shifted at Alexander's command. On this, see also Sélincourt (1958) and Ferrill (1985).

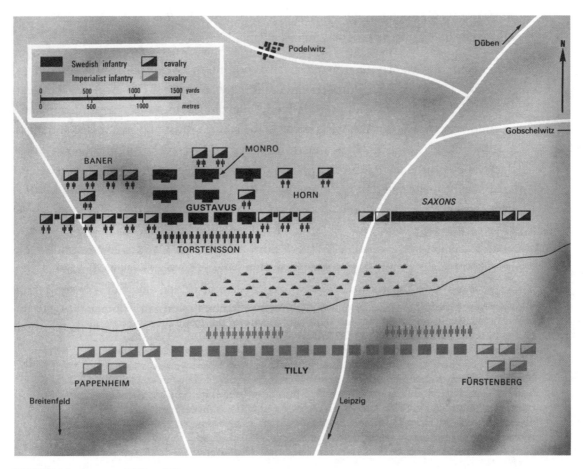

SOURCE: Montgomery, 1968, p. 272.

Figure 2—The Massed Armies of Breitenfeld

Air warfare, too, would move from the melee to mass. Airpower pioneer Billy Mitchell himself noted that the Germans, late in World War I, did begin to move systematically away from the melee, toward massed formations. As he put it: "The Germans . . . sent their machines over in a mass . . . which were able to go anywhere they desired against the smaller forces of the French" ([1928] 1960, p. 152). After World War I, significant improvements were made in both the range and payload of aircraft. The rise of radar and radio also made tactical and strategic command and control of large air forces possible.

All these advances hinted at the rise of a distinct form of war from the air, which many thought would change the nature of conflict (DeSeversky, 1942; Douhet, 1942). And every theorist of airpower expounded on the importance of mass, both for achieving maximum bombardment effects, and for the security of the aerial force itself. Indeed, one of the lead bombers of this era, the B-17, bristled with machine guns and was dubbed the "Flying Fortress" precisely because of the security it was thought to enjoy in close-massed squadron "box" formations. The use of airpower in World War II and even in

Korea and Vietnam—although in these cases to a lesser extent—also represented the dominance of the principle of massing (see Pape, 1995).

In the realm of social conflict there was also movement away from wild melees in the streets and fields to more controlled and coordinated activities. The difference between the chaos of social conflict during the French Revolution and the synchronized social revolutions of 1848 across Europe is perhaps the best contrast between melee and mass. In 1848, the telegraph enabled the revolutionaries to achieve unprecedented mass effects—both at the tactical level, by enabling crowds larger than ever before to assemble at specified sites, and at the operational level, by enabling a coordination of mass effects across large geographic areas, including beyond the borders of several states. However, massing alone could not overturn the existing European social order—just as massing on land and sea led to deadlock during World War I, and massed bomber formations suffered mightily during World War II. It would take further developments in the nature of massing, as eventually epitomized by Leninist doctrines, but also something more to unleash the ultimate potential of mass: the emergence at the social level of the third basic form of conflict, maneuver. It had ancient origins, but its evolution quickened in the 1700s and came to fruition in the 20th century.

Maneuver Warfare

- **Basic characteristics**
  - **Complex, synchronized, fast-tempo, multi-linear operations to surprise, penetrate, flank**
  - **Application of mobile mass at "decisive point"**
- **Enabling technologies: electronic comms (esp. radio)**
- **Historical cases**
  - **Land: Roman maniples, to German panzers**
  - **Sea: Nelson at Trafalgar; Togo at Tsushima**
  - **Air: Stuka support of blitzkrieg operations**
  - **Social: Mexican Revolution, Russian Revolution**

The key elements of maneuver include complex, synchronized movements of entire forces, most often at a high operational tempo. The desired goal is to enlarge the battle-space well beyond the fixed limits imposed by mass-on-mass engagements, posing the prospect of massing selectively against small portions of the enemy forces—preferably, at what Clausewitz ([1831] 1976) and Jomini ([1838] 1992) both referred to variously as the "decisive point" upon which the adversary's continued cohesion depended. Maneuver of this sort entails using multiple axes of advance as well as flanking movements to generate surprise and penetration of the enemy "front."

Maneuver has been around since ancient times. It has, under skillful leadership (e.g., Alexander, Genghis Khan, Turenne, and Napoleon in his early years), sometimes been briefly ascendant over massed brute force. But, over the past century-plus, maneuver has grown to be generally superior to massing. This state of affairs has been brought about in large part by the rise of electronic communications—especially radio. Radio allowed the battlespace to be greatly expanded, turning armed forces into "sensory organizations" as well as fighting units. This combination of sensing and shooting enabled the emergence of doctrines of hitherto unimagined complexity and speed, and was deepened by the new information technology of radar, which came into its own during the

1920s and 1930s—and which would make World War II, with its far-flung maneuver campaigns, so different from World War I.[7] The invigorating effects of the new information technologies also opened the possibility of compromising the enemy's information security, so as to be able to anticipate maneuvers and thwart them. Indeed, under code names like Ultra and Magic, such information operations played crucial roles in both the European and Pacific theaters during World War II (on this, see Kahn, 1993; Prados, 1995).

But we should not forget that maneuver has early origins. The supple checkerboard formation of the Roman maniples (literally "handfuls") enabled swift, complex tactical movements, making the legions virtually unbeatable for centuries. Yet, few other examples stand out in such stark contrast to mass-oriented warfare—with the exception of the Mongols of the 12th and 13th centuries—at least until the emergence of Frederick the Great's "oblique order" of battle, perfected over many years of campaigning, always at a numerical disadvantage, from the 1740s to the 1760s. Perhaps the greatest expression of this Prussian way of war was seen in the Battle of Leuthen in 1757, when Frederick's army of 36,000 took on 80,000 Austrians. Clearly, mass alone would not suffice. The Prussians won a stunning victory by achieving the ultimate aim of maneuver: application of superior mass against a portion of the opposing force, leading to the disruption of the rest of the enemy army. In a day of hard fighting, Frederick's "right hook" at Leuthen did just that (see Figure 3).[8]

About 25 years after Leuthen, British Admiral Rodney would do at sea what Frederick had done on land. He would deviate from the long-held "fighting instructions" of the Royal Navy, which enjoined all to maintain the mass of the "line of battle." Instead, he took part of his forces, maneuvering them so as to strike at a small portion of his French opponents. His victory at the Battle of the Saints (in the West Indies), foreshadowed Lord Nelson's more systematic development of naval maneuver principles, which would be so brilliantly executed during the Napoleonic wars, culminating in the Battle of Trafalgar in 1805. Napoleon himself would observe, years later while in his final exile, that it was British advantages in communications (the Hopham flag-hoist system) that were the key to the defeat of the French navy. One hundred years after Trafalgar, Japanese Admiral Togo would employ similar Nelsonian maneuver principles to defeat the Russian Navy at Tsushima—yet another battle in which the management of information allowed complex maneuvers to be coordinated at (relative to the time) high speed.[9]

---

[7]On the importance of the electronic revolution during this period, see Page (1962).

[8]For a detailed description of Prussian maneuver doctrine, see Frederick's "Military Instructions," edited and translated by T.R. Phillips (1943).

[9]For Napoleon's views, see De Chair (1992, pp. 124–125). See Mahan (1890, 1894) for analysis of naval maneuver from Rodney to Nelson. Hough (1958) provides an insightful account of Tsushima.

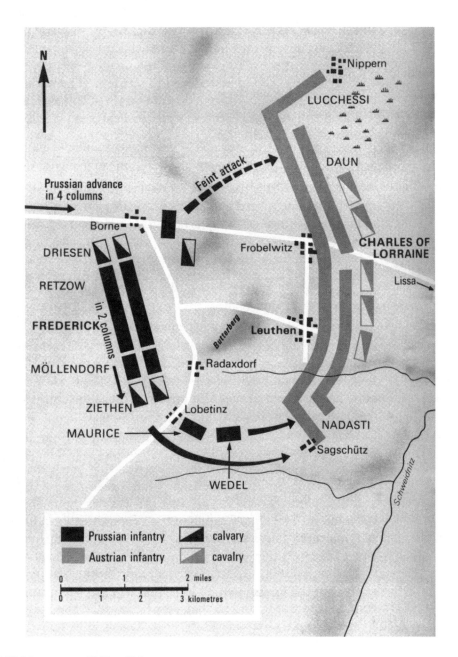

SOURCE: Montgomery, 1968, p. 326.

Figure 3—Frederick's Maneuver at Leuthen

The emergence of maneuver in the aerial realm can be seen most clearly in the integration of ground attack aircraft with mobile armored forces in what became known as blitzkrieg. Indeed, this form of war, featuring the close coordination of air and ground forces, raised maneuver to a dominant place as a doctrine, beginning with the Battle of

France in 1940[10] and the invasion of Russia in 1941, and culminating 50 years later in the signal victory over Iraq won by American and British mobile maneuver ground forces—which were as dependent upon airpower as the panzer divisions of half a century earlier. Indeed, in the Gulf War case, the reliance upon airpower was so great that seven weeks of aerial bombardment preceded mobile ground operations.[11]

Another major effort to use airpower as a means of facilitating maneuver consisted of operations aimed at air-dropping ground forces at chosen points in the battlespace. The problem with this was that such drops necessarily entailed keeping the ground troops light (i.e., absent artillery and tanks), resulting in costly engagements for the airborne troops since they often had to face superior firepower. In World War II, the German invasion of Crete and the Allied airdrop on Arnhem are both examples of the costly consequences of this form of war. Later on, air maneuver with helicopters was tried, with similar results for the Americans in Vietnam and for the Russians in Afghanistan—even though, in these latter two cases, both heliborne protagonists were able, because of their air supremacy, to airlift in some heavier weapons (generally artillery).[12]

At the level of social conflict, advances in information technologies and organizational methods had similarly powerful effects. Whereas, during the 19th century, social activism and revolution evolved from melees to massing, in the 20th century complex maneuver strategies began to emerge, under skillful guidance from leaders aware of their growing ability to mass selectively at points and moments where the governments they opposed were weak. Thus, although the social revolutions of 1848 all failed, the Mexican and Russian Revolutions of the early 20th century, occurring but a few years apart, were wildly successful. These revolutions involved an emphasis on the creation of mass organizations that could hold mass demonstrations, but they were also the harbingers of "maneuver-oriented" social revolutions that would, in coming decades, help bring about the downfall of colonial empires and the rise of both totalitarian and theocratic (i.e., largely Islamic) regimes. One of the best cases of "social maneuver" was Gandhi's nonviolent campaign to undermine British rule in India. This last example, although it reflects the selective massing—in the Indian case, for strikes and protests—that goes with maneuver, is also replete with (successful) efforts to overwhelm the whole British system of colonial governance on the subcontinent—and may thus be thought of as a case that involved "swarming" as well.[13]

---

[10]On the origins of blitzkrieg, see Guderian (1957) and Addington (1971). On the importance of close coordination of tanks and ground attack aircraft during the Battle of France, see Mellenthin (1956, pp. 17–18), who notes that the crucial attack at Sedan "could not hope to succeed unless the French artillery was eliminated." He then observes that "the Stuka onslaught completely silenced the French artillery, making victory possible."

[11]Some of the reasoning in favor of this lengthy bombing had to do with the hope that it would have the coercive effect of inducing the Iraqis to withdraw from Kuwait—obviating the need for a ground attack.

[12]The emergence of the concept of heliborne "vertical envelopment" is chronicled in Maclear (1981, pp. 181–206) and critically analyzed in Sorley (1999).

[13]On Gandhi's strategic approach, see Collins and LaPierre (1975).

Emerging Way of Fighting: Swarming

- **Basic characteristics**
    - **Autonomous or semi-autonomous units engaging in convergent assault on a common target**
    - **Amorphous but coordinated way to strike from all directions—"sustainable pulsing" of force or fire**
    - **Many small, dispersed, internetted maneuver units**
    - **Integrated surveillance, sensors, C4I for "topsight"**
    - **Stand-off and close-in capabilities**
    - **Attacks designed to disrupt cohesion of adversary**

- **A real possibility? Too big a leap? How to depict?**

Swarming requires complex organizational innovations and more information structuring and processing capabilities than do the earlier paradigms (melee, massing, and maneuver). While the notion of a "swarm" conjures up an image of attackers—from bugs to bombers—striking a target from every direction, it is less clear whether swarmers should operate autonomously or follow some controlling authority. In nature, swarms are composed of independent units whose actions are largely instinctual. In human conflict, swarms may be either independently targeted or guided. For example, the Vietcong attacks during the Tet Offensive in 1968, while ordered by Hanoi, enjoyed a very large degree of freedom of action—in line with Mao's strategic dictum of "strategic centralization, tactical decentralization" (Griffiths, 1961, p. 114). Conversely, during the World War II Battle of the Atlantic, German U-boat wolfpack attacks that converged on convoys were tightly controlled by Admiral Doenitz's direct orders (see Doenitz, 1959).

The key active process of the military swarm is "sustainable pulsing," of either force or fire. By this we mean that swarmers will generally take their positions in a dispersed fashion—much like U-boats on patrol. Then, they will be able to come together, concentrating their force or fire, to strike at selected targets from all directions. After a strike, they will be able to redisperse—not only to blanket the battlespace but also to mitigate the risk posed by enemy countermeasures—ready to "pulse" to the attack again, as circumstances permit. This should not be thought of as a strictly military phenomenon. Sustainable pulsing can be undertaken in social action as well. As seen from time to time in Serbia, those protesting the Milosevic regime's nullification of local elections a few years ago, for example, were able to assemble in very large numbers on many occasions. A similar effort is under way by civil society actors in Serbia now.

Swarming has two fundamental requirements. First, to be able to strike at an adversary from multiple directions, there must be large numbers of small units of maneuver that are tightly internetted—i.e., that can communicate and coordinate with each other at will, and are expected to do so. The second requirement is that the "swarm force" must not only engage in strike operations, but also form part of a "sensory organization," providing the surveillance and synoptic-level observations necessary to the creation and maintenance of "topsight." Thus, swarming relies upon what Libicki (1994) calls "the many and the small," as well as upon Gelernter's (1991) notion of a command element that "knows" a great deal but intervenes only sparingly, when necessary. These two fundamental requirements may necessitate creating new systems for command, control, communications, computers, and intelligence (C4I).

Even though the rise of precision-guided munitions heralds an era in which stand-off weapons have come into their own, we must emphasize that our notion of swarming can be carried out by either fire or force. Swarming from afar, through directed fire, may sound most appealing, but it is likely that swarming "close-in" will still be quite common. Swarming in force will probably be seen mainly in low-intensity conflicts, as in the operations of the Chechens during their 1994–1996 war against the Russians (see Arquilla and Karasik, 1999). But it may be especially evident in peacekeeping and/or peacemaking operations. The "blanketing" swarm of U.S. forces in Haiti in the wake of the American intervention stands out as a signal success. A capacity for swarming in force is perhaps the best hope today for keeping the peace in Kosovo—even though such a capacity is lacking and apparently is not being cultivated.

The Haiti and Kosovo examples speak implicitly to the point that swarming in force may depend very much on local friendliness. When fighting takes place in populated areas—as opposed to a swarm-permissive desert theater with little local population to be concerned with, such as was featured in the Gulf War—goodwill may matter quite a bit. Haitians were and Kosovars would have been very accepting of the presence of U.S. forces. Haitians did and Kosovars would have provided valuable information to the swarmers. But a swarming force operating amid a hostile people would have difficulty moving undetected. More generally, it reflects the need to consider the conditions under which swarming will be more achievable and effective. It may turn out that swarming operations will be easier to mount when on the defensive, when one is more assured of fighting on friendly terrain (e.g., see the swarming Soviet anti-tank networks that played such a brilliant role in defeating the German blitzkrieg in the Battle of Kursk).[14]

The ultimate aim of a swarm may be less the physical destruction of an enemy—although much damage can be done—and more the disruption of its cohesion. Once deeply disrupted, the enemy will lose his ability to maneuver or fire effectively, and the military aims of the "swarm force" will come readily to hand. A good illustration of the disruptive power of a swarm can be seen in the military operations of the Zulus during the 19th century. Fast-moving Zulu *impi,* capable of marching over 40 miles per day, would break into small units as they went into the attack, surrounding their opponents and swiftly destroying their cohesion. This was swarming in force on a grand scale and was quite different from the flanking movements common in maneuver warfare because the weight of a Zulu attack was roughly equally distributed *at all points.* For decades, their way of war proved unassailably effective, and a great Zulu empire rose. Ultimately, the Zulus clashed with the Europeans; and they even gave hardy Boer commandos and British regular forces—both armed far better than they—a close run in the war of 1879 (Morris, 1965, is the definitive study of the Zulus).

Is swarming a realistic possibility as the next major fighting doctrine? Can it supplant the apotheosis of maneuver, AirLand Battle? Should it? Or is this too high a goal? Will Clausewitz's "friction" and the fog of war prove intractable obstacles to swarming? Finally, how can swarming be conceptualized and depicted in ways that allow for doctrinal development and, ultimately, its practice? This last question must be asked and answered before any assessment of the potential merits of swarming can be judged. Fortunately, the analytic task is eased a bit by the presence of swarming both in nature and, episodically, in earlier history. An examination of these antecedents follows in the next chapter.

---

[14]For a detailed discussion of the problems posed by these antitank networks, see Carell (1966). He notes the great importance the Red Army gave to proper training for this new way of blunting the German panzer attacks: "For weeks on end [before the battle], the Russian troops had been trained in antitank tactics by *experienced tank officers*" (p. 29). Emphasis added.

Chapter Three

INSTANCES OF SWARMING

Swarming in Nature

- **Bees, ants as exemplary metaphors**
  - **Hive organization: deploy by "blanketing," then mount linear, omnidirectional attacks**
  - **Like guerrillas, activist groups**
- **Wolves, hyenas also instructive**
  - **Pack organization: mobile small units**
  - **Like U-boats, "soccer hooligans"**
- **Flies, mosquitoes, sharks as variants**
  - **Opportunistic mobbing—each one for itself**
  - **Like paparazzi**
- **Viruses, bacteria, antibodies**

Swarming appears in the animal kingdom, long before it does in human affairs. Military swarming cannot be modeled closely after swarming in the animal kingdom. But some useful lessons and insights may be drawn from it. In nature, several different types of swarming take place, and several organizing principles enable such behavior to be sustained.

The first form of swarming occurs in "hive" or "nesting" types of organizations, best exemplified by bees, ants, and some other species of social insects (Wilson, 1971). Typically, these insects employ "blanketing" tactics when foraging outside the hive or nest, striking at their adversaries or prey from all directions. The goal is to overwhelm any cohesive defenses that might be mustered. Although these insects often move in linear formations, they are quite adept at shifting into a swarming mode at the point of engagement. In the case of ants, this behavior has been called "swarm raiding" (see Hölldobler and Wilson, 1994).

Ants differ from bees and other social insects in that they employ swarming not only in pursuit of food, or in immediate defense of the hive—but also in extended territorial wars against other ants. These wars are frequently protracted, and of an operational complexity that mirrors human wars in striking ways. As Hoyt (1996, p. 199) puts it, "ants were going to war long, long before . . . the first recorded human wars were fought almost six thousand years ago." The swarming of ants also differs from other insects in that ants, armed with powerful mandibles and some acid-spraying capability, sustain their behavior throughout an engagement, and over an entire campaign (see Gotwald, 1995; Schneirlea, 1971). Bees, on the other hand, have individuals that can swarm just once, as the act of stinging results in the stinger's own death. In this respect, ant "swarm raids" may provide a more useful model of what we call the "sustainable pulsing" of forces—while bees may resemble more the swarming of fire, as their stinging deaths seem analogous to "fire-and-forget" precision-guided munitions.

The swarming pattern of these social insects resembles guerrilla tactics in some ways, with linear formations used for movement, then omnidirectional, blanketing "wave" attacks at the point of contact. This was certainly the pattern of engagements in Vietnam—both during the French and American periods of involvement. In operations other than war, the blanketing notion can also be glimpsed from time to time. Instructive recent examples can be found in the American intervention in Haiti, as well as in the Mexican Army's deployment to Chiapas against the Zapatistas (see Ronfeldt et al., 1998). In both cases, blanketing was employed for deterrent purposes, so as to set up an "omnipresence" that cowed insurgents into military inactivity. Social activist movements, too, often follow a similar pattern of engagement. The Chicago riots at the Democratic convention in 1968 provide a good example of this phenomenon, in that the swarming "Yippie" march to the Chicago Loop gave way to fighting in which police found themselves beset from all directions (Royko, 1971, p. 183).

The second form of organization that fosters swarming in nature is found among animals that move in packs. Wolves and hyenas are prominent in this class, which features small, mobile units—as opposed to the large insect swarms. Such packs often take up semi-dispersed formations, coming close together only in the final stages of swarming attacks on weakened members of target herds. The goal is to isolate a particular victim, cutting it out from the massed security of its own group. This tactic also has seen application in guerrilla warfare—both in the operations of the Spanish guerrillas against French supply trains in the Peninsular War, and in Mao's ability to "cut out" small elements of Kuomintang forces and decimate them during the Chinese Civil War. The success of predators that use pack tactics is dependent on both their ability to run for extended periods (allowing the dispersal of the group) and on their organization and voice communications (which enable swarming at the critical moment in the hunt). Lorenz (1966, p. 130) even noted, among wolves, what appeared to be a brief "meeting" of the pack—including touching of noses—just prior to the moment of the final attack.

The best example of military pack-like organization is no doubt the U-boat campaign of World War II. Subsequent to World War I, the submarine was greatly improved technologically. Its "running" capacity was extended with improved diesel engines, and its sensing and communications capabilities were vastly improved by advances in radar and radio (see Doenitz, 1959; and Brodie, 1943). We will discuss this in more detail in our survey of 20th century military swarming.

Social conflict also features pack-like organizations, as exemplified by modern-day "soccer hooligans." They generally operate in a loosely dispersed fashion, then swarm against targets of opportunity who are "cut out" from a larger group of people. The use of modern information technologies—from the Internet to cell phones—has facilitated plans and operations by such gangs (see Sullivan, 1997). A recent example of the power of this kind of group is in Serbia, where the political opposition to Milosevic has tried to mobilize soccer hooligan groups to strike at police who might attack or threaten demonstrators opposing the regime.[15]

A third form of swarming in nature features what we call "mobbing." Again, there is the notion of overwhelming assaults on an intruder or foreign object. But there are two variants. Mobbing can either be opportunistic—i.e., with each seeking its own gain, as with non-hive insects like mosquitoes (see Evans, 1984; and Wootton, 1984)—or mobbing can serve a common goal, such as breaking down or defending an immune system—as in the everyday fight between viruses, bacteria, and the various antibodies that strive to hold them at bay. Indeed, the swarming of antibodies provides a powerful metaphor for thinking about securing information against predatory electronic attacks by computer viruses (see Kephart, 1994; and Forrest et al., 1994). Apart from insects and viruses, sharks provide yet another good example of opportunistic mobbing—as do the frenzied actions of modern-day paparazzi.

---

[15]Alex Todorovic, "Serb Opposition Taps Soccer Fans as a Force for Change," *The Christian Science Monitor,* September 21, 1999, p. 7.

Swarming In Military History

- **In the ancient world**
    - **"Parthian shots" as form of swarming by fire**
    - **Small Athenian Navy swarms forces at Salamis**
    - **Byzantine heavy cavalry swarm via fire and force**
    - **Mongols swarm fire (horn bows) and force (horses)**
- **In the era of nation states**
    - **Drake's "sea dogs" defeat Spanish Armada**
    - **American Minutemen rout British regulars**
    - **Italian *carbonari* vs. Austrian occupation**
    - **U.S. Cavalry and Indians swarm in Plains Wars**
    - **Zulus' early victories over British regulars**

In the ancient world, swarming was a common approach to battle employed by mounted archers. The horse granted mobility and the bow gave an added capacity for fire at "stand-off" range. This was an ideal approach to war for nomadic tribes, which practiced swarming in their countless raids upon and wars with more settled civilizations. But this way of war was not limited to stateless wanderers—the Persian Empire also adopted it as a favored doctrine. Best known for the Parthian horsemen, who could fire while riding away from an onrushing opponent (the "Parthian shot"), the Persians were able to conquer a vast Middle Eastern empire, one that Alexander the Great conquered only after developing his cavalry's own counterswarming capabilities (see Fuller, 1960; and Edwards, 2000). The Persians recovered their empire soon after Alexander's death, continuing their military tradition of swarming—later using it to destroy the Roman legions of Crassus. But they would meet their match in the Byzantines, who learned to emulate Parthian doctrine and did so with armored cavalry who could swarm with fire or in force (Delbrueck, [1921] 1990; and Graves, 1938).

Swarming was evident in ancient warfare at sea as well, the best example being the Battle of Salamis in the second Greco-Persian War (fought over a century-and-a-half before Alexander). The Persians were striving to bring Greece under their imperial control by sending a large expeditionary force and supporting navy to invade Attica in 480 B.C.

Ultimately, they reached as far as Athens, at which point the Athenians abandoned their city for the island of Salamis—and relied on their navy to defeat the Persians. The Greeks were outnumbered at sea by over three to one; but their vessels were small and agile, and the battle was fought in narrow waters. As Themistocles, the Athenian naval visionary foresaw, greater maneuverability would allow the Greeks to strike at the Persians from all directions simultaneously, throwing them into confusion and negating their numerical advantage. The Greeks thus won a signal victory—using swarming—against a seemingly superior foe (Rodgers, 1937; Jordan, 1975; and Starr, 1989, pp. 32–34). Interestingly, the Japanese used a similar swarming approach at sea to defeat the second attempted Mongol invasion of Japan in 1281—albeit with an assist from a typhoon, after weeks of fighting (see Japanese views of the invasion in Sansom, 1958; and Farris, 1996).

While the Mongols failed in their invasion of Japan, they were nevertheless the absolute masters of swarming in land warfare. They combined the mobility of the horse with the rapid, long-range fire of their horn bows to create an imposing ability to swarm either fire or forces. To this capability they added a very decentralized organizational structure that gave great leeway to local commanders. They also feigned retreats, often luring their opponents into loosening their battle formations while "in pursuit"—only to turn and swarm upon them at a propitious moment. Finally, their Arrow Riders assured the swift flows of important information, allowing an overall commander to have a very clear idea of just what his widely distributed swarming forces were up to (see in particular Curtin, 1908; and Chambers, 1985). Many centuries would pass before other militaries would begin to acquire the kinds of capabilities that the Mongols demonstrated in their heyday in the 13th and 14th centuries.[16]

In the period from the Protestant Reformation, in the 16th century, to the early industrial era 300 years later, swarming made only fitful appearances. Most professional militaries opted for traditional mass and maneuver formations—but some instances in which it appeared were very important to the future course of history. The best example of this is the British naval resistance to the Spanish Armada in 1588, a campaign that saw a decisive shift toward the swarming of fire in naval warfare. The British strategy was to strike with stand-off fire at many points along the line of Spanish vessels trying to make their way up the English Channel. Repeatedly, the Spaniards strove in vain to close with the British, hoping to use their edge in numbers of sailors and soldiers to board and take the Royal Navy vessels. They failed, and in the war that dragged on in the wake of their aborted invasion, the British would build on their capability for swarming, calling together their "sea dogs," from time to time, to strike out against the far-flung bastions of the Spanish Empire, one at a time. Sir Francis Drake was a principal developer of this strategic approach to swarming (see Thomson, 1972; Cummins, 1995).

---

[16]For a discussion about the Mongols as organizational and doctrinal precursors of "cyberwar," see Arquilla and Ronfeldt (1993).

The British would find themselves on the receiving end of the next great episode of swarming, during the American Revolution. Beginning with the battles of Lexington and Concord in 1775 (Fischer, 1994),[17] and continuing in varying degrees throughout the war, Empire forces would find themselves time and again trying to use their linear doctrine against opponents who were often operating in small, dispersed units that would come together as the occasion arose, to swarm their fire against the easy target provided by the mass-minded British Army. Despite the continuing effort of American forces to emulate massed, linear, European models of warfare, the embryonic U.S. Army would eventually draw important, enduring lessons about the value of resorting to omnidirectional, aimed fire by small groups (Weigley, 1973; Millett and Maslowski, 1994).

Other interesting uses of swarming in "wars of liberation" were the guerrilla efforts in Spain against French occupation during the Napoleonic wars (1808–1814) and the resistance of the Italian *carbonari* to Austrian control of Italy in the 1820s and 1830s. The Spaniards—whose whole population supported the resistance to occupation—were wildly successful at "pulsing" their strike forces consistently against carefully targeted French supply columns, while the Italians failed to win freedom from Austria by this means. Lewis Gann argued (1970) that the Spaniards did well because the local geography favored them, and because the British gave them a great deal of support—including with a standing field army operating under Wellington out of Portugal. The Italian resistance, on the other hand, had no outside sponsorship, and fared poorly (on this, see also Ashley, 1926, pp. 56–57).

Later in the 19th century, swarming would also fail in some colonial wars between advanced militaries and tribal opponents. For example, in 1879, the Zulus, after a few heady successes of swarming in force, were eventually defeated by the British advantage in fire (Morris, 1965). However, the Native Americans of the Great Plains developed a very good capacity for swarming, hit-and run fire against columns of settlers or cavalry, and gave a very good account of themselves in the Plains Wars of the 1870s (see Wellman, 1992).

In sum, the experience of swarming, as it has occurred in conflicts prior to the 20th century, has generally been good. There have been some striking successes (e.g., the Greeks at sea; the Mongols on land), while the failures can often be attributed to technological (in the case of the Zulus) or numerical (for the Plains Indians) deficiencies. Interestingly, these last two cases are almost the only historical examples of the defeat of swarming forces that fought on their own ground and enjoyed the strong support of their own people. This earlier historical experience offers encouraging evidence of the usefulness of swarming; but it should be noted that we had to search far and wide to find even these cases (for additional documentation, see Edwards, 2000). Swarming was not a prevalent

---

[17]Stephen Vincent Benét (1944, p. 35) was the first to note that the "colonists *swarmed* from their houses like angry bees and shot down the red-coated men from behind stone walls" (our emphasis added).

mode of conflict prior to the 20th century. For professional military organizations and officers almost everywhere, the decisive incentives accrued to the development of bigger institutional hierarchies and weapon systems, in eras when information and communications systems were improving but still remained quite slow, centralized, and cumbersome—all of which favored the continued development of mass and maneuver approaches to warfare. And, as we shall see, swarming made only fitful appearances even in this century of "total wars."

Swarming in the Industrial Era

- **War in the 20th century**
  - **German U-boats were dispersed, pulsed to attack, then dissevered, recombined**
  - **Fighter command won Battle of Britain with defensive swarming, drawing on radar**
  - **Japanese kamikazes in the Pacific**
  - **Chinese PLA in Korea (1950)**

✔ **Britain has had the most extended exposure to and experience with swarming, on offense and defense**

When the leading powers shifted away from colonial warfare to fighting with each other, they soon found themselves embroiled in the bloodiest fighting in the history of the world. In World War I, the mass-industrial mode of warfare led to shocking attrition on both sides, with both victors and vanquished suffering grievously. None of the combatants was able to employ substantial maneuvers along with more direct mass attacks (see Liddell Hart, 1930; Keegan, 1998). By the time of World War II, the rise of mechanization allowed for a great deal of maneuver; but mass warfare still reigned, and attrition remained decisive in most theaters of the war. Ellis (1990) has argued that it was simply a victory of "brute force," while Dyer (1985, p. 88) has observed that

> [n]o innovation stays a surprise for very long, and by the middle of the war, when German forces were fighting deep inside the Soviet Union, attrition had returned with a vengeance. The solution to the blitzkrieg tactic of rapid penetration was to make the defended zone deeper—many miles deep, with successive belts of trenches, minefields, bunkers, gun positions, and tank traps which would slow down the armored spearheads and eventually wear them away. Sometimes the defense would hold; sometimes there would be a successful breakthrough, but even then, the continuous front would not disappear. It would roll back some dozens of miles or hundreds of miles all along the line and then stabilize again.

Despite the persistence of mass-based, attritional warfare in an age of mechanization, there were instances of odd new forms of maneuver in which lines or fronts meant little, and where battle formations were mostly dispersed, massing only occasionally—in short, where something that could accurately be called swarming took place. The clearest and most sustained example of swarming in World War II was the U-boat war. It commenced on the first day of the war in 1939 and ended on the last day of the war in 1945. The German submarines deployed in widely dispersed fashion, coming together to swarm convoys that were spotted trying to make the passage across the Atlantic. There were no fronts in this fight. There was only the dogged, often failing, effort to fight off the U-boats' "pulsing" to the attack, then dissevering only to recombine later to resume their assaults.[18]

In the end, the U-boats were finally beaten by improved means of detection of their movements—including aerial surveillance, high-frequency direction-finding equipment and, finally, wireless communications intercepts (see Winterbotham, 1974, pp. 83–103; and Kahn, 1993). As the development of the snorkel allowed U-boats to steam faster and farther while remaining submerged, offsetting the Allies' air surveillance efforts somewhat, it was really what should be seen as "information operations" (direction finding and decryption) that won the Battle of the Atlantic.

While the U-boats were offensive swarmers, some defensive swarming also arose during World War II. This occurred principally in efforts to deal with massed strategic bombers. The first such effort was mounted by the British Fighter Command, formed late in the 1930s—just in time to play a decisive role in the Battle of Britain. The concept of operations was simple: Radar would be used to provide warning of the size and direction of a German attack, then word would go out to widely dispersed air bases, from which the defenders would swarm to the attack. Over a period of months, this swarming defense decisively defeated the German Luftwaffe (Deighton, 1977; Wright, 1969; and Wood and Dempster, 1961). The Germans themselves strove to emulate the British swarming methods—and did so with much success (see Galland, 1973).[19] The British—now joined by the Americans—focused on information flows as the key to swarming and pioneered both modern electronic warfare and some aspects of information warfare in their efforts to counter German defenses.[20]

---

[18]Donald Macintyre, who commanded Allied convoy escort forces during the war, provides perhaps the best detailed description (1971, pp. 122–137) of the U-boats' methods of swarming—and how to counter them—in his account of the "painful losses" suffered in the week-long struggle of Convoy HG76.

[19]Adolf Galland was a fighter pilot who ultimately masterminded German defensive strategy against the Allied bombing campaign. Bekker (1967) draws extensively from official German documents to outline the efforts taken to emulate the British approach to air defense. Tactically, though, the Germans were even more innovative, because their fighters employed four-plane Schwarm formations, in which both horizontal and vertical dispersion were featured—a striking contrast to the three-plane tight vees practiced by the British and Americans.

[20]On the rise of electronic warfare to support the air war against Germany, see Jones (1978). For a German perspective on the so-called "wizard war"—and its effects, see the memoirs of Germany's then Inspector General of Fire Prevention, Hans Rumpf (1962).

As for the use of airpower for tactical offensive swarming during World War II, the best example is provided by the Japanese kamikaze attacks on U.S. Navy vessels—especially in the struggle for Okinawa (see Feifer, 1992, pp. 195–229), where American casualties from kamikaze attacks came close to those incurred in the ground fighting.[21] Overall, during the last two years of the Pacific War, the Japanese used nearly 1,300 "Zero" planes in kamikaze roles. These attacks resulted in the sinking of 34 U.S. Navy vessels and the serious damaging of 288 more. First described in Hector Bywater's eerily prescient (1925) novel about a future war between the United States and Japan, kamikaze tactics consisted of simultaneously descending upon an enemy ship or ships from multiple directions, in theory—and often in practice—overloading the defense of the target vessel. Save for the presence of a human pilot, the kamikaze doctrine seems quite like the naval missile tactics that emerged in the 1970s and 1980s (see Hughes, 1986).

By way of contrast with the kamikazes, Allied fighter-bombers during the Battle of France in 1944 were able to swarm without engaging in suicidal attacks. Instead, they relentlessly patrolled over the battlefield, constantly reporting on German force concentrations and coming together repeatedly to deal disruptive blows (see Figure 4). These fighter-bombers played a crucial role in preventing or delaying reinforcements from arriving during the seven weeks of hard fighting prior to General Patton's breakout from Normandy. These swarms of fighter-bombers next acted defensively, stopping the German counterattack at Mortain, and went back on the offensive, swarming once more over the exposed German panzers and infantry caught in the Falaise pocket—what has come to be called "the killing ground" (Carell, 1960; and Blumenson, 1963). In this respect, the swarming air operations during the Battle of France in 1944 should be seen as the genesis of the devastating allied air swarms that were to decimate Iraqi forces during the Gulf War—as allied air forces prowled relentlessly over the battlefield, then converged upon Iraqi concentrations and columns time and again.

After World War II, the Chinese People's Liberation Army's (PLA's) intervention in the Korean War late in 1950 also featured a great deal of swarming—U.N. forces found themselves, again and again, surrounded by North Korean and Chinese forces that "packetized" themselves and infiltrated well beyond any recognized front—then attacked from all directions. The most dramatic example of a running fight with a hostile swarm is the retreat of the First Marine Division from the Chosin Reservoir (see especially Russ, 1999; and Hastings, 1987, pp. 128–146). While U.N. forces ultimately dealt with these swarming tactics, they were highly effective in rolling back the Allied forces from the Yalu

---

[21]Both Feifer (p. 573) and Keegan (1989, p. 573) agree that American battle deaths due to ground combat totaled about 7,000, while kamikazes killed over 5,000 sailors in attacks that sank 38 ships of all sizes, and damaged many more—including task force commander Admiral Raymond Spruance's flagship, which lost 396 men as a result of kamikaze attack. This near equivalence in losses is especially significant in light of the extreme savagery of the ground fighting, which saw the commanding generals on both sides killed in combat. Kamikazes made the sea fight just as bitterly fought.

Frank Wootton, detail of *Rocket Firing Typhoons at the Falaise Gap, Normandy, 1944,* courtesy of the Imperial War Museum, London.

Figure 4—RAF Swarming at Falaise

River—and the argument has been made that this type of fighting might prove to be a very effective way of fighting against a modern mechanized army in the future (see Alexander, 1995).

In summary, swarming appeared intermittently in the major wars of the 20th century. Only once did it lead to a decisive victory in an important campaign: the Battle of Britain in the fall of 1940. But in each of the other cases, from the U-boat war to the Korean War, swarming always had powerful tactical and operational effects—even the suicidal kamikaze attacks of the Japanese inflicted grievous losses.

Perhaps these cases herald an era in which swarming can become more effective. If so, it may prove particularly useful to study the military experiences of the British. Britain has had more exposure to and experience with swarming, on both offense and defense, than any other actor. During World War II, the Royal Air Force formulated an air defense based on swarming, and then the Royal Navy coped with German swarming attacks at sea. Earlier, the British Army faced a great deal of swarming from colonial and tribal adversaries. Nor should it be forgotten that the British pioneered a kind of swarming in their long war with Spain in the 16th century, starting with operations against the Armada and culminating in a series of powerful swarming strikes against far-flung Spanish holdings around the world.

In recent decades, swarming has begun to emerge more frequently, and to be practiced by a wider variety of actors. In what follows, insights will be drawn from this broader experience, helping to provide a basis for doctrinal development.

Recent Examples of Swarming—
By Fire and Force

	By Fire	By Force	
In Major Theater Wars			
ARG AF in Falklands	+	++	
U.S. airpower in Gulf	+++	+	
In Vietnam			
VC/NVA		+++	**+** Little swarming
U.S. Army	+++	+	
In Afghanistan			**++** Some swarming
Red Army	+++	+	
Mujahideen	+	+++	**+++** A lot of swarming
In Chechnya			
Chechens	++	+++	
Russians	+	+	
Stability Operations			
U.S. in Haiti		+++	
Aidid in Somalia		+++	
Social Netwars			
Zapatistas	+++	+	
Battle of Seattle	+	+++	

Much of the military swarming that emerged during World War II could be found in air operations. This remained true in the postwar period, when airpower came of age and played a crucial role in the outcome of land and naval campaigns. The U.S. Air Force's role in the Gulf War has already been alluded to as a textbook case of the swarming of fire, even though most (about 90 percent) of the ordnance dropped on the Iraqis was composed of "dumb" rather than smart bombs (Hallion, 1992). During the South Atlantic War for the Falklands, fought in 1982, the Argentine (ARG) Air Force was even more reliant on dumb weapons, compelling its pilots to approach quite close to the Royal Navy vessels that they were targeting. Despite heavy losses, the Argentinians were able to press home lethal swarming attacks that made the whole campaign—for the British—a "near run thing" (see Hastings and Jenkins, 1983; and Cordesman and Wagner, 1990).

During the Vietnam War, a great deal of what can indisputably be called swarming went on. While the communist forces had little ability to swarm fire, their battle tactics, when on the offensive against American firebases, clearly adopted the notion of striking from all directions, intermingling themselves as closely as possible with the enemy so as to minimize the effects of hostile artillery and air strikes. These swarming attacks extended from the gathering together of widely distributed maneuver units, which would dissever and redisperse after completion of the attacking phase of operations. The American response was to fight along the lines of what Maclear (1981, pp. 181–206) has called "Westy's War"—General William Westmoreland's effort to use swarming air and artillery fire to catch the communist forces whenever they were concentrated. Thus, in its swarming aspects, the Vietnam War was one in which the swarming of force by the North Vietnamese Army (NVA) and Vietcong (VC) was opposed by American fire swarms. On the battlefield, the loss-exchange-ratios tended to favor U.S. forces (Sorley, 1999)—but of course there was much more to this war than what transpired on the battlefield. Indeed, one could write an entire report just on the social swarming of protesting elements of the American public, and their effect on overall support for continuation of the war.

Interestingly, a similar pattern of swarming operations emerged during the Russian War in Afghanistan (1979–88); the Red Army relied heavily upon fire and the mujahideen more on the concentration of swarming forces. Both sides did try, from time to time, to branch out. Russian special forces occasionally tried to attack insurgent forces in a swarming manner (i.e., in an omnidirectional way); and the mujahideen did take advantage of the rough, mountainous terrain of Afghanistan to create "Stinger traps" for Russian jets and helicopters. These were appropriately named, because the Stinger shoulder-mounted antiaircraft weapons would fire from all directions upon enemy aircraft that strayed into their fire traps. And, in retrospect, it seems that the mujahideen swarm attacks by fire, although far less frequent than their ground operations, were highly effective at curbing Russian airpower and dominance (Cordesman and Wagner, 1990). Finally, it should also be noted that both in Afghanistan and Vietnam, swarmers fought on their home terrain and enjoyed the overwhelming support of their people.

Russian military woes worsened during the first war in Chechnya (1994–96), when the Chechens' clan-based social networks employed swarming to a substantial degree. The Chechen forte was to attack in small bands (12–20) of fighters from all directions. These bands would "pulse" to the attack, then dissever and recombine for future attacks—a classic swarming pattern. The Chechens also had large amounts of rocket-propelled grenades and shoulder-mounted antiaircraft weapons, enabling them to mount fire swarms almost as often as they swarmed their forces (see Lieven, 1998; and Gall and de Waal, 1998). The Russian Army, on the other hand, seemed to have learned little since the war in Afghanistan and scarcely engaged in any swarming. Instead, it approached the war on the ground in a linear fashion, focusing on capturing ground rather than engaging Chechen forces under advantageous conditions. Russian use of airpower was also unimaginative, and therefore ineffective. However, the Russian troops themselves fought with great valor and learned much from the fighting. They should be expected to do better—ultimately—in the current troubles in Chechnya—as well as in future engagements with Chechen armed fighters (on this point, see Arquilla and Karasik, 1999).

At the level of military operations other than war, there have also been a number of instructive examples of the swarming of force in recent years—each involving the U.S. military. In Haiti, the American military was able to maintain societal order by "blanketing" the countryside during the period of intervention. This prevented outbreaks of unrest. U.S. forces deployed all over the area of operations and quickly responded in a swarming fashion to any signs of trouble. Swarming of force was employed also in Somalia—although this time the swarming came from clan leader Mohammed Farah Aidid. In the major engagement during this involvement, in October of 1993, hundreds of Somali "technicals" engaged the American Task Force Ranger and inflicted serious losses on U.S. forces. Even though Aidid's own troops suffered far more, enough damage was done to the Americans that a groundswell of U.S. public opinion arose, calling for an end to intervention in that troubled land (see Bowden, 1999).

A recent example of swarming can be found in Mexico, at the level of what we call activist "social netwar" (see Ronfeldt et al., 1998). Briefly, we see the Zapatista movement, begun in January 1994 and continuing today, as an effort to mobilize global civil society to exert pressure on the government of Mexico to accede to the demands of the Zapatista guerrilla army (EZLN) for land reform and more equitable treatment under the law. The EZLN has been successful in engaging the interest of hundreds of NGOs, who have repeatedly swarmed their media-oriented "fire" (i.e., sharp messages of reproach) against the government. The NGOs also swarmed in force—at least initially—by sending hundreds of activists into Chiapas to provide presence and additional pressure. The government was able to mount only a minimal counterswarming "fire" of its own, in terms of counterpropaganda. However, it did eventually succeed in curbing the movement of activists into Chiapas, and the Mexican military has engaged in the same kind of "blanketing" of force that U.S. troops employed in Haiti—with similar success.

In summary, a wealth of swarming has transpired in the past few decades. Some cases have been very successful (e.g., American air operations in the Gulf; Chechen insurgents). Some of it has been problematic (e.g., the U.S. military's fire swarms in Vietnam). An interesting pattern is the tendency, in those conflicts with major military operations, for the more advanced power to rely upon fire swarms, while the less advanced combatant has employed swarming in force. While this seems intuitively logical behavior for both sides, the unexpected point is that the swarms of force have done better than those of fire (e.g., Vietnam, Afghanistan, and Chechnya). And even in lower-intensity settings, swarming of force has been highly effective (e.g., in Haiti and Chiapas).

This is a theme worth watching, because conventional wisdom regarding the revolution in military affairs (RMA) has coalesced around a belief in the ability to achieve remarkable results with weapons fired from stand-off range. This brief review of the past few decades suggests that close-in capabilities may prove to be as, if not more, important than the ability to strike targets from a distance. At a minimum, this insight suggests that advanced militaries may need to reexamine their close-in fighting capabilities and doctrines, since some types of conflicts, particular irregular ones, may limit the usefulness of stand-off weapons—and militaries do not always get to choose the type of war in which they become engaged.

Lessons from a Review of History

- **Swarming has long played a role in warfare**
  - **Most effective for small, dispersed, mobile units that are internetted, have topsight**
  - **In many cases, small forces defeat large ones**
  - **Seldom deliberately developed as doctrine**
- **Scattered efforts to formulate swarm-like doctrines**
  - **Bakunin's anarchistic "general strike" theory**
  - **Churchill's "special operations executive"**
  - **Mao's concepts about "people's war"**
  - **Heilbrunn's idea of "concentric dispersion"**

Swarming has been around since ancient times, sometimes even playing an important role in warfare. For the most part, mass and maneuver have dominated the landscape of conflict. But on those occasions where swarming has made a difference, its practitioners have enjoyed advantages in mobility and stand-off fire—against conventionally configured enemies—especially when good communications and decentralized organizational structures allowed information to be acted upon in a timely fashion.[22] Ancient and medieval mounted armies, from the Parthians to the Mongols, had all these traits. In the more modern era, the U-boat campaign and defensive air operations against heavy bombers during World War II also featured these characteristics—with these operations providing an even clearer exposition of the principle of wide dispersion in deployment, then "pulsing" repeatedly to the attack.

When swarming worked, it worked very well, often acting as a tremendous force multiplier. The Mongol "hordes," for example, generally fought against numerically superior foes. Swarming also triumphed over far superior numbers when the Greek Navy defeated the Persians at Salamis in 480 B.C., and the Japanese held off the Sino-Mongol inva-

---

[22]There are no good earlier historical examples of a swarming doctrine employed against guerrilla forces—which may themselves disperse widely so as to vitiate the effects of swarmed fire. Against guerrillas, swarming in force may be preferable, although this will depend upon whether the local populace supports the guerrillas or the counterguerrilla swarmers.

sion of 1281 A.D.—for seven long weeks before the typhoon season came, with its "divine wind" (see Yamada, 1916). In the 20th century, the early swarming "wolfpack" tactics of a few U-boats came very close to bringing the British Empire to its knees. The lesson seems clear: Swarming can be a way for relatively small, mobile, internetted forces, operating with superior topsight, to optimize military effectiveness, even when the balance of forces runs against the swarmers.

Despite this evidence, or perhaps because these cases are so few and far between, swarming has never been systematically and explicitly developed as a major doctrine. But there have been important scattered efforts to recognize the value of swarm-like approaches to conflict. The most clearly developed theoretical work on the subject can be found at the level of social conflict. In anarchist thought, for example, the "general strike" theory of Mikhail Bakunin focused on the notion of pulsing the power of workers in simultaneous strikes aimed at bringing down the state. As E. H. Carr put it, Bakunin used his general strike theory as a means of overwhelming the state, a "conception of revolution through the people by destroying the power of the State" (1950, p. 101). His approach is strikingly different from classical revolutionary thought, which instead keys on ways to *seize* state power and use it in ways that are often ultimately beneficial to the state itself (Skocpol, 1979).

At a more directly military level, Winston Churchill, during the darkest days of World War II for Britain, outlined a strategy that would strike at the Nazis from virtually all directions. It depended on the skillful employment of small, dispersed bands of commandos and resistance fighters. Ironically, his inspiration for the "special operations executive" was derived from the debacle at Dunkirk, as he noted in a letter to General Ismay of the War Cabinet:

> What we have seen at Dunkirk shows how quickly troops can be moved off (*and I suppose on*) to selected points if need be. How wonderful it would be if the Germans could be made to wonder where they were going to be struck next, instead of forcing us to try to wall in the island and roof it over! An effort must be made to shake off the mental and moral prostration to the will and initiative of the enemy from which we suffer (1949, p. 243, emphasis added).

Defeat may be a powerful motivator, for in the case of Mao Zedong, his views on People's War, a concept that prominently features what we call swarming, also grew out of early failures on the conventional battlefield. He emphasized the value of small, dispersed units that were nonetheless still operating under a guiding strategic vision (1961). The success of People's War doctrine, first in China over Kuomintang forces, then against French and later U.S. forces in Vietnam, suggests that the impact of swarming in the 20th century has actually been substantial.

A few decades after People's War was developed, German strategist Otto Heilbrunn (1965) advanced a systematic vision of military swarming. He was attempting to deal with the problem of how to improve the survivability of conventional military forces on the tactical nuclear battlefield. His answer consisted of a new set of smaller units of maneuver and a doctrine based on the principle of what he called "concentric dispersion." The idea featured his small, dispersed units held together with robust communications networks that only come together ("pulse," to use our term) at the point and time of attack. After the attack, they would swiftly break off, redisperse, and continue their separate but coordinated movements until the next attack—or they could concentrate defensively to deal with an attacker.

We intend to use these disparate strands of thought as additional building blocks in our effort to illuminate the prospects for a future doctrine for information-age conflict across the spectrum—from social activism and operations other than war to high-intensity, major theater warfare. Further, since the historical examples of swarming are drawn from all dimensions of conflict, our hope is that a doctrine of swarming will be applicable on land, at sea, or in the air—and across a variety of types of terrain, including built-up areas.

Looking Ahead

- **Conditions for swarming are increasing**
  - **Emerging as major mode of military, social conflict**
  - **Enabled by information operations**
- **U.S. will increasingly face swarming by adversaries**
  - **Across conflict spectrum, more LIC in near term**
  - **Useful both on offense and defense**
- **U.S. military should develop own swarming doctrine**
- → **To develop a doctrine, must attend systematically to bundles of organizational and technological issues**

The information revolution and advances in information operations in particular are giving swarming an opportunity to diffuse across much of the spectrum of conflict. Indeed, the phenomenon of swarming is likely to have overarching effects on military affairs in the coming years. And its development will be driven not only by the U.S. armed forces but also by a host of potential adversaries, coming from a variety of lesser states to "peer competitors." Beyond nation states, swarming is also likely to prove valuable to terrorist and transnational criminal organizations, as well as to clan-based ethnonationalists. Even militant NGOs and other civil society actors will find swarming a useful means for engaging as well as constraining the United States.

Looking across the spectrum of conflict, we sense a likelihood that swarming will be featured more often in the low-intensity conflicts (LICs) of the near future. It is a natural doctrine for networked organizations to apply, and the most networked groups extant are those operating at the nonstate level. Swarming is also attractive because of the ease with which those who apply it can shift from offense to defense, and vice versa. The Chechen bands of fighters that defeated the Russian Army in the 1994–96 war used swarming both offensively and defensively—and were highly effective at both (see Arquilla and Karasik, 1999).

The rise of swarming on both offense and defense will likely be swift, especially among nonstate antagonists, since the barriers to entry for new practitioners are low and its usefulness as an offset to conventional U.S. hard power is potentially quite high. For these reasons, the U.S. military would be well advised to proceed ahead now with the development of a swarming doctrine of its own. If the military does not do so, the risks may grow that American soldiers will—one day soon—be caught by a kind of doctrinal surprise.

As to how best to proceed with the process of doctrinal development, we would emphasize the importance of the organizational aspects of swarming and the need to "bundle together" organization and technology, so that advances in one are geared to advances in the other. This is likely to be especially true when thinking about the new technologies that can help swarming actualize its potential. We must not lose sight of the organizational-technological nexus of progress—to explore the new technologies without clear new concepts of operations and organization is to risk wandering in a labyrinth.

Chapter Four

Military Swarming Design Elements— A Recapitulation

- **Many small, dispersed, internetted maneuver units**
- **All-service coordination for mixing and matching**
- **Both stand-off and close-in capabilities**
- **Integrated surveillance, sensors, C4I for "topsight"**
- **Aim: "sustainable pulsing" of force and/or fire**
- **Result: amorphous but coordinated way to strike from all directions—stealthy ubiquity, no "front"**
- **Tenet: centralized strategy, decentralized tactics, distributed formations and logistics**

Swarming—a seemingly amorphous, but deliberately structured, coordinated, and strategic way to strike from all directions, by means of a sustainable pulsing of force and/or fire, close-in as well as from stand-off positions—will work best, and perhaps will only work, if it is designed mainly around the deployment of myriad, small, dispersed, networked maneuver units (what, below, we will call "pods" organized in "clusters"). Swarming cannot work if it is based on traditional mass or maneuver formations. These swarm units are not only internetted with each other, but also can coordinate and call upon other assets in the area. To achieve this, swarming depends upon the operation of a vast, integrated sensory system that can distribute not only specific targeting information but also overall topsight about conditions in and around the battlespace.

A military that wants to conduct swarming, either of fire or in force, will have to habituate itself to the devolution of a great deal of command and control authority to a large number of small maneuver units. These units will be widely dispersed throughout the battlespace and will likely represent all the various sea, air, and ground services—putting a premium on interservice coordination for purposes of both sharing information and combining in joint "task groups." Such formations should be capable of rapidly fielding a swarm either of stand-off fire or of close-in combat forces (which may have their own as well as supporting fire available).

It seems clear that this doctrinal vision cannot be effected in the absence of a fully integrated surveillance and communications system. The vision must help turn the military into a "sensory organization," while the system will be crucial for internetting the operational units. The command, control, communications, computers, intelligence, surveillance, and reconnaissance (C4ISR) system may generate so much information that it will be necessary to come up with new ways to segregate the often time-urgent need of the operational unit from the higher command's need to retain clear "topsight" (Gelernter, 1991)—a "big picture" view of what is going on.

If the informational needs of a swarming military force can be fulfilled, then it will be possible to undertake the "signature" act of a swarm: the "sustainable pulsing" of forces and/or their fire. This essential notion consists of the ability to repeatedly strike the adversary—with fire or force—from all directions, then to dissever from the attack, redisperse, and repeat the cycle as battle conditions require. If this can be achieved, then the military employing such a doctrine will surely pose a host of nettlesome problems for mass-oriented forces. First, the swarm force will be far more stealthy, since its order of battle will be characterized by amorphousness, at least to the eyes of the enemy. The small size and dispersed deployment of its units of maneuver will help to convey an image simultaneously stealthy and ubiquitous—a kind of "stealthy ubiquity." Thus the force will be largely unseen and undetectable,[23] but it will be able to congeal and strike decisively anywhere in the battlespace—with no limitation imposed by lines or fronts. Indeed, there may be no "front" per se. This, we believe, is the potential of a swarming force, whose basic tenets must be to pursue centralized strategic control while at the same time decontrolling tactical command, dispersing units, and redesigning logistics.

The most difficult task may be to craft logistical practices that make sense on a widely distributed battlespace in which friendly and enemy forces are intermingled. A swarming force, quite simply, places demands on logistics that differ sharply from the prevailing practices of the past 350 years, which have always emphasized the provision of mass munitions, transport, and manpower (Van Creveld, 1977). For swarming, these goods and services will have to be delivered not to fixed locations, but to an ever-shifting set of small forces almost all constantly on the move. Solutions to this problem are beyond the scope of this study—but we highlight this crucial question, and observe a few mitigating points. First, the swarming forces will likely be far smaller than a traditional expeditionary force that consists, say, of a field army (400,000+ troops), some aircraft carrier battlegroups, and half a dozen air wings (400+ aircraft). A swarm force may, under opti-

___

[23]Difficulties may arise in the case of trying to engage in swarming in an area where the opponent is fighting in guerrilla fashion and enjoys the support of the local populace. We are grateful to Bevin Alexander, who has emphasized this point in discussions with us—and whose own study (1995) of the future of conflict examines this issue in detail.

mal circumstances, comprise as little as a tenth of the usual number of ground forces—a lesser quantitative demand, in absolute terms, which may help resolve the logistical challenges of swarming.

So, while supplying a swarm may require wholly new thinking about the means of distribution, the smaller size of the swarm may mean that the amount of supplies that have to be delivered will be much lower. This diminished need for mass quantities may also allow for a host of new means of delivery to be considered and developed. But before the logistics and other aspects of swarming can begin to be fully worked out, it is first useful to think through the initial modeling of a system based on swarming.

Theoretical Models of Swarm Systems*

- **Autonomous agents**
- **With high (but not too high) connectivity**
- **Relying on basic rules, instructions**
- **Interacting in fluid, shifting networks**
- **No centralized control—no "hub"**
- ✔ **About "flocking" as much as "swarming"?**
- ✔ **Instructive but limited applicability to real life?**

*Kevin Kelly, *Out of Control*, 1994; writings about Swarm model since 1993 (www.santafe.edu and www.swarm.org).

Some preliminary theorizing has been done on swarm systems (e.g., Kelly, 1994, mentions "swarm networks" and discusses other patterns of behavior that pertain to swarming). Further, in such places as the Santa Fe Institute and the Center for Naval Analyses, efforts have been under way in recent years to model and simulate the behavior of various kinds of swarm systems. Indeed, theorists associated with the Santa Fe Institute have developed a sophisticated software package, really a toolkit, called SWARM for doing simulations that, although mainly relevant for studying artificial life, have resulted in some economic and military modeling applications as well.[24] New ideas are also being researched about the emergence of a collective "swarm intelligence" in both natural and artificial systems (see Bonabeau, Dorigo, and Theraulaz, 1999).

This theoretical and experimental work usually depicts swarming as a system in which autonomous agents interact and move around according to a set of rules and a schedule, often seeking an optimal outcome vis à vis another agent, set of agents, or environmental feature. The modeling allows for continual interactions among the agents, as they form and reform in fluid, shifting networks (and maybe hierarchies as well). These networks may persist for some time, or may break down and recombine into others oppor-

---

[24]See materials at http://www.swarm.org/. Also see the simulations known as "ISAAC" by Andrew Ilachinsky, available at the web site of the Center for Naval Analyses, http://www.cna.org/isaac/.

tunistically. Information may flow quite freely from one agent to the next about conditions near them in the model, but, in the examples we have seen, there is rarely an identifiable distribution of, or hub for distributing, topsight among all the agents. Some of the models and applications seem to be more about follow-the-leader or follow-your-neighbor "flocking" behavior than swarming conjointly to attack an adversary or other target.

According to our literature survey, the main theoretical/experimental work being done on swarming today does not have much overlap with what we mean by swarming. The SWARM toolkit is powerful and adaptable. It could be used to simulate what we mean by swarming (including BattleSwarm, a concept introduced later), but so far, to our knowledge, none of its applications have moved in this direction.

New work needs to be done for such models to address real conflict situations—from social activism to high-intensity warfare—in which swarming is present or might be used. And the models may have to be substantially different from those that currently exist. For example, it is not at all clear that real military swarm forces will be—or should be—fully autonomous or lacking in central strategic control. This might create inefficiencies in the allocation of fire or might foster a practice of "overmassing" at those times when swarming in force is called for. Someone must—it seems in the military case—retain topsight. To do this, without succumbing to the temptation to overcontrol events in the field, may become an essential element of information-age generalship.

Swarming in Practice

- **Civil-society NGO activism resembles theory well**

- **Some terrorist, criminal groups resemble theory**

- **Business, military practices differ most from theory**
  - **Limited autonomy of agents/units**
  - **Variations in connectivity**
  - **Rules and instructions not so simple**
  - **Explicit networks: chain, hub, all-channel**
  - **Hybrids of hierarchies and networks important**

As swarming emerges across the spectrum of conflict, theory and practice will go through a dialectic. At present, the practice of swarming appears to be ahead of theory; certainly there are many cases of swarming in real life that have yet to be analyzed and used for theory building. But as new theoretical and philosophical treatments arise, they will surely be used to reshape the strategies and tactics of swarming's practitioners.

At present, our best understanding of swarming—as an optimal way for myriad, small, dispersed, autonomous but internetted maneuver units to coordinate and conduct repeated pulsing attacks, by fire or force—is best exemplified in practice by the latest generation of activist NGOs, which assemble into transnational networks and use information operations to assail government actors over policy issues. These NGOs work comfortably within a context of autonomy from each other; they also take advantage of their high connectivity to interact in the fluid, flexible ways called for by swarm theory.

The growing number of cases in which activists have used swarming include, in the security area, the Zapatista movement in Mexico and the International Campaign to Ban Landmines (ICBL). The former is a seminal case of "social netwar," in which transnationally networked NGOs helped deter the Mexican government and army from attacking the Zapatistas militarily.[25] In the latter case, a netwar-like movement, after getting

---

[25]On the concept of "netwar," see Arquilla and Ronfeldt (1996). On the Zapatista case, see Ronfeldt et al. (1998), and Cleaver (1998a,b).

most nations to sign an international antilandmine treaty, won a Nobel Peace Prize.[26] Swarming tactics have also been used, to a lesser degree, by pro-democracy movements aiming to put a dictatorship on the defensive and/or to alter U.S. trade and other relations with that dictatorship. Burma is a case of this.[27]

Social swarming is especially on the rise among activists that oppose global trade and investment policies. Internet-based protests helped to prevent approval of the Multilateral Agreement on Investment (MAI) in Europe in 1998.[28] Then, on July 18, 1999—a day that came to be known as J18—furious anticapitalist demonstrations took place in London, as tens of thousands of activists converged on the city, while other activists mounted parallel demonstrations in other countries. J18 was largely organized over the Internet, with no central direction or leadership.[29] Most recently, with J18 as a partial blueprint, several tens of thousands of activists, most of them Americans but many also from Canada and Europe, swarmed into Seattle to shut down a major meeting of the World Trade Organization (WTO) on opening day, November 30, 1999—in an operation known to militant activists and anarchists as N30, whose planning began right after J18. The vigor of these three movements and the effectiveness of the activists' obstructionism came as a surprise to the authorities.

The violent street demonstrations in Seattle manifested all the conflict formations discussed earlier—the melee, massing, maneuver, and swarming. Moreover, the demonstrations showed that information-age networks (the NGOs) can prevail against hierarchies (the WTO and the Seattle police), at least for a while.[30] The persistence of this "Seattle swarming" model in the April 16, 2000, demonstrations (known as A16) against the International Monetary Fund and the World Bank in Washington, D.C., suggests that it has proven effective enough to continue to be used.[31]

From the standpoints of both theory and practice, some of the most interesting swarming was conducted by black-masked anarchists who referred to themselves collectively as the N30 Black Bloc, which consisted of anarchists from various affinity groups around the United States. After months of planning, they took to the field individually and in small groups, dispersed but internetted by two-way radios and other communications

---

[26]On the ICBL, see speeches by Jody Williams (e.g., her speech accepting the Nobel Peace Prize in 1997 and a speech she gave at a gathering of Nobel laureates at the University of Virginia in 1998, posted at http://www.virginia.edu/nobel/transcript/jwilliams.html).

[27]On Burma, see Danitz and Strobel (1999, 2000).

[28]On the MAI, see Kobrin (1998).

[29]The observations about J18 come mainly from an ITN (International Television Network) news report, November 1, 1999, based on reportage by Mark Easton of Channel Four News and made available subsequently at ITN Online. This is the kind of publicly available reportage that could have given accurate early warning to Seattle's police and mayor of the demonstrations they would soon face.

[30]The best analysis of the N30 protest demonstrations in Seattle, from a netwar perspective, is by De Armond (2000a, 2000b).

[31]One of the authors, in an interview with well-placed members of the Direct Action Network, which helped coordinate the Battle of Seattle, was told that the concept of swarming was a central element in their approach—and would continue to be used because of its effectiveness.

measures, with a concept of collective organization that was fluid and dynamic, but nonetheless tight. They knew exactly what corporate offices and shops they intended to damage—they had specific target lists. And by using spotters and staying constantly in motion, they largely avoided contact with the police (instead, they sometimes clashed with "peace keepers" among the protesters). While their tactics wrought physical destruction, they saw their larger philosophical and strategic goals in disruptive informational terms, as amounting to breaking the "spell" of private property, corporate hegemony, and capitalism over society.[32]

In these social netwars—from the Zapatistas in 1994, through the N30 activists and anarchists in 1999—swarming appears not only in real-life actions but also through measures in cyberspace. Swarms of email sent to government figures are an example. But some "hacktivists" aim to be more disruptive—pursuing "electronic civil disobedience." One notable recent effort associated with a collectivity called the Electronic Disturbance Theater is actually named SWARM. It seeks to move "digital Zapatismo" beyond the initial emphasis of its creators on their "FloodNet" computer system, which has been used to mount massive "ping" attacks on government and corporate web sites, including as part of J18. The aim of its proponents is to come up with new kinds of "electronic pulse systems" for supporting militant activism.[33] This is clearly meant to enable swarming in cyberspace by myriad people against government, military, and corporate targets.

Meanwhile, uncivil society actors, such as transnational criminals and terrorists, are also showing proclivities for swarming. In the U.S.-led drug war, for example, a great emphasis has been placed on targeting the leaders of criminal cartels. But because today's drug cartels are networked and dispersed, rather than operating under any sort of central command, drugs continue to be swarmed into the United States unabated—in small amounts packetized on the backs of illegal immigrants along the southwest border and in scads of small shipments delivered by truck, small boat, and plane at locations all over the "battlespace."

Various terrorists are proving adept at networking and, in some cases, swarming.[34] For example, Hizbollah uses a swarming approach to deal with Israeli commando raids in southern Lebanon. This approach is based on a general instruction to Hizbollah's widely distributed units to converge—like antibodies, it seems—on any intruders in a given area. No central leadership is required, and Israeli commandos—themselves not swarming, but rather trying to engage in "precision strikes" on specific, limited targets—have found themselves more than once facing swarming attacks from which they escape but only with serious loss. The inability of the Israeli military to deal with these Hizbollah

---

[32]The observations in this paragraph stem mainly from a communique circulated on the Internet by the ACME Collective, which is associated with the N30 Black Bloc.

[33]Interested readers should visit http://www.nyu.edu/projects/wray/ and related web sites.

[34]For more detailed discussion of terrorist networking and swarming, see Lesser et al. (1999, especially pp. 39–84), Zanini (1999), and Arquilla, Ronfeldt, and Zanini (2000).

swarms may even have contributed to Israel's recent unilateral withdrawal from southern Lebanon.

"Al Qaeda," or "the Base," as Osama bin Laden's terror network is known, may be trying to engage in "strategic swarming"—an effort to strike simultaneously, or with close sequencing, at widely separated targets (e.g., the embassy bombings in Kenya and Tanzania). But, so far, his ability to mount operations of strategic significance seems limited. Also, to the extent to which the Base's operations depend upon bin Laden's direct leadership, this is a case that differs from the "leaderless" quality of classic swarm theory.

As an aside, we note that swarming is even showing up in the sports world, by way of professional basketball's successful "triangle offense," pioneered by Tex Winter in the 1940s and honed by Phil Jackson, first with the Chicago Bulls in the 1990s and now with the Los Angeles Lakers. This offense is based on keeping the players dispersed (about 15–20 feet apart) and arrayed in a series of triangular formations (similar to mini-all-channel networks). The movement of the players then continually creates new triangles, as the players try to pass or move around the defense. If the defenders are able to hold up the progress of one triangle, then player movement creates another triangle, partly composed of members of the first. The system is fluid, shifting, and an excellent means of swarming opposing teams from all directions—allowing any offensive player to shoot, depending on how the swarm flows.[35]

However, in two other areas where networking and swarming are beginning to occur—commercial and military affairs—conditions diverge greatly from the theoretical swarming paradigm in almost every dimension. For example, business and the military rarely allow full autonomy, given the consequences of individual misfeasance. Long ago, for example, Admiral Byng was shot for deviating from the Royal Navy's *Fighting Instructions* and losing strategically valuable Port Mahon during the Seven Years' War (Mahan, 1890, pp. 286–291). Recently, a single broker's free-wheeling actions caused losses in the billions, bringing down the two-hundred-year-old Baring's, Limited, a scion of British investment banking. Clearly, in both commerce and war, costs and risks are high, so much so as to inhibit notions that full autonomy can ever be enjoyed by units "in the field."

In the area of connectivity, businesses and militaries also stand apart from pure notions of swarming. There are, in practice, wide variations in connectivity among units, in part to maintain strategic control, in part out of bureaucratic institutional interest. However, there are exceptions; for example, the U.S. Navy's concept of "network-centric warfare" would allow for a great deal of connectivity—and a lot of decentralization of decision-

---

[35]We are grateful to Bevin Alexander for pointing out that hockey and soccer also feature distributed formations conducive to swarming—as opposed to football, which emphasizes coordination in close-knit, massed configurations.

making authority. The Marine Corps, in its Hunter Warrior/Sea Dragon experiments (which we discuss in detail at a later point), is also moving toward ever greater connectivity.

Furthermore, the "rule sets" in business and military affairs tend to be exceedingly complex, compared to those in the models of swarming described above. Also, to the extent to which networking is emerging, explicit structures are preferred—limiting the fluid and shifting quality of the models in favor of easy-to-recognize chain, hub, and even some all-channel network forms.[36] Lastly, the institutional need—in businesses and militaries—for unity of purpose and strategic vision drives both forms of endeavor to seek to have hybrid organizational structures, in which some sort of networking is grafted to existing or redesigned hierarchical forms. This will pose daunting design challenges to commercial or military organizations that want to move toward a capability for swarming.

---

[36]See a discussion below of these network forms.

Organizational Design Challenges

- Moving a "large-unit" military to small units
  - Daunting logistical, medical, C2 challenges
  - Balancing specialized, multipurpose functions

- Networking inherently hierarchical structures
  - What kinds of networks? Hybrids?
  - How much connectivity? Control/decontrol?

- Creating new fighting formations: pods, clusters?

What lies behind the fact that so many NGOs are ahead of military actors when it comes to networking and swarming is not so much the adaptability of the NGOs to the technologies of the information revolution, but rather to the organizational innovations it affords. Indeed, the primary challenges for military institutions in moving to swarming will be more organizational than technological.

For militaries, the challenge of changing from the "large and the few" to the "small and the many" (see Libicki, 1994, pp. 19–51, for a thorough exposition of these phrases) is very steep. The army corps, the aircraft carrier battlegroup, as well as the air expeditionary force—all these are big and are designed to be big enough to fight a major theater war (e.g., the Gulf War of 1990–91). They are also quite self-contained enterprises in the operational, logistical, and communications spheres. And, since the rise of the all-purpose divisional structure over 200 years ago (see Black, 1994), "big" has generally worked well—perhaps with the exception of some guerrilla and other irregular wars (e.g., Vietnam) where "big unit" warfare foundered badly.[37] Basically, the predilection for "few and large" military formations has been around for centuries and has tended to function reasonably well. These inertial factors alone suggest the likely difficulties in encouraging radical "downsizing" of combat forces.

---

[37]On the fits that irregular forces have given big militaries, see Gann (1970). Krepinevich (1986) examines the wrongheadedness of the big-unit approach during the Vietnam War.

In addition to the inertial forces at play, there is the added problem that shifting to the "small and the many" may cause nightmares for combat support functions. We have already discussed some of the connectivity and logistical hurdles and the mitigating factors in these issue areas. Beyond the supply and communications realms, however, lie such issues as the medical functions. Where on the wide-open, nonlinear battlespace do the wounded go? Where do mobile surgical units set up shop? To some extent, the field medics will have to upgrade their skills considerably—and they may need to be aided by distant, on-line support and real-time consultation.[38] But the loss of more soldiers, as a percentage of those wounded, seems a real risk (operationally and for morale) in moving to a small, nimble swarming force. There would seem to be very little hope of achieving the high survival rate for wounded that was sustained between 1965–1973 in Vietnam— over 80 percent (Sorley, 1999, p. 43). But that was a losing war with heavy casualties. A swarming campaign should incur far fewer losses, overall, and have higher winning chances—in almost all types of conflict. Finally, it may be that the approach taken (e.g., tilt-rotor aircraft like the Osprey) to providing swarming forces with tactical mobility in the first place—i.e., for their infiltration and exfiltration from various points—may also mitigate the problem of medical evacuation.

Existing military structures tend to be able to serve multipurpose functions. Even a heavy U.S. armored division has some battalions of infantry; and an aircraft carrier battlegroup has both surface warfare missile ships as well as antisubmarine and submarine assets. And air expeditionary forces have all manner of platforms, from heavy bombers to fighters and aircraft capable of suppressing ground fire and/or providing close support to maneuver forces in the field. Would moving to a military of the "many and the small" jeopardize or compromise this multipurpose way of war?

It might—at least in terms of ground forces. It is hard to see how very small units (say, of platoon size) could ever call themselves "heavy." But the real issue is whether "heaviness" is a virtue in itself—or can it be replaced or compensated for by swarms of supporting fire from air and naval assets? If so, then small ground forces might well be able to take on much heavier opponents. There is also the risk that, in an age of acute sensing capabilities, the heavier one's military is, the harder it will fall to the fire of precision-guided munitions. Nevertheless, it is important to recognize that the shift from few and large to many and small reduces the need for organic all-purpose units, and places a premium on networking with other forces capable of replicating—perhaps exceeding—the firepower lost by the shift.

The implication is that the downsizing of militaries (e.g., the U.S. military drew down its manpower by about one-third during the 1990s) can work well, if it goes hand-in-hand

---

[38]Carell (1966, p. 20) notes that the Germans thought deeply about the problem of caring for casualties on a distributed battle site—such as they confronted in the Soviet antitank networks at Kursk—and chose to attach surgical teams directly to their assault forces at the company level. The experiment proved very successful in terms of saving the lives of the seriously wounded. Due to shortages in medical personnel and the almost complete shift to the defensive after Kursk, this experiment was not repeated on any significant scale for the duration of the war.

with the rise of networks to supplant traditional hierarchical structures. This begs the question of just what sorts of networks should be formed, and what kinds of hybrids of hierarchies and networks might work well in the military context. Further, there are questions about how much interconnectivity military units should have. Should they know as much as the theater commander? Probably not. But they should probably know much more than traditional junior officers have ever known about the battlespace. This, of course, highlights the issue of the degree to which command authority should devolve to lower levels. Where hybrids of networks and hierarchies seem an appropriate design, a skillful blending of control and decontrol should help to solve or mitigate the authority issues raised by institutional redesign.

What will the actual fighting units look like in the age of swarming? At sea and in the air, we see no immediate need for undergoing a major change in hardware. Naval and air warfare can move to swarming—largely of fire—principally on the basis of organizational rather than technical redesign. Ground forces, on the other hand, simply cannot swarm if the Army remains structured as it is, designed to cope mainly with a full-scale mass armored invasion on the plains of Western Europe. In our view, there will need to be a major shift to light fighting vehicles—away from tanks.[39] Light strike vehicles would form the basis "pod"—what we foresee as the basic unit of maneuver in swarming. Beyond this, pods would group into "clusters" by working conjointly with their physically nearest and most integrated fellow fighters in the field.

We shall elaborate on pods, clusters, and the new doctrine they imply in what follows. Prior to doing so, however, we must describe and analyze the networking options available to them. For the success of swarming by the "small and the many" will be a function of the power of their networking. Even if a devotion to tanks persists, our large number of tank-less formations will be greatly empowered by swarming. No longer will senior planners view light forces as sacrificial "speed bumps" when they have to be deployed quickly to hold off heavily armored foes—as was the case in the Gulf during the buildup against Saddam Hussein. Swarming will give these light forces a lethal punch to deal with even the heaviest opposition.

---

[39]Alexander (1995) and Friedman and Friedman (1996) have also articulated the case for moving away from armor—but without recommending the kind of radical redesign of military organizational forms that we believe must accompany a shift away from tanks. Also, a swarming force has less need of tanks as a means of breaking through enemy lines or concentrations—the initial purpose for the British creation of tanks (see Liddell Hart, 1930, p. 118). Finally, we note that the current ten divisions of the U.S. Army already feature four that have no tanks whatsoever (see Heyman, 1999, for detailed listings).

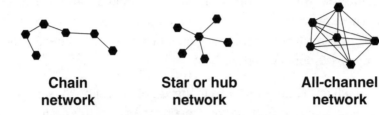

Basic Types of Networks: Building Blocks of the New Formations

Chain network   **Star or hub network**   **All-channel network**

- **Each type suits different purposes, situations**
- **All-channel gives network form its high potential**
- **Mixes of all three may be present, advisable**

In an archetypal swarm force, the units are likely to resemble an array of dispersed, inter-netted "nodes" set to act as an "all-channel network." The challenge for swarmers is to gain a better understanding of the nature of networks, the design options, and their applicability to military warfare. During recent cases of social swarming—e.g., the series of mobilizations known as J18, N30, and A16—activists formed into very open, all-channel network designs whose strength depended in part on free-flowing discussion and information-sharing. But such transparency may be impossible for military swarmers who depend on stealth and secrecy; cellular network designs may be imperative for them.

As the scholarly literature instructs, networks come in basically three major types (or topologies):

- the *chain* or line network, in which people, materials, or information move along a line of separated contacts, and where end-to-end communication travels through the intermediate nodes

- the *star*, hub, or wheel network, in which a set of actors are tied to a central (but not hierarchical) node or actor and must go through that node to communicate and coordinate with each other

- the *all-channel* network, in which everyone is connected to everyone else.

Each design is suited to different conditions and purposes. Of the three, the all-channel network is the most difficult to organize and sustain, partly because of the dense communications it may require. But it is the type that gives the network form its new, high potential for collaborative undertakings. It is the type that is gaining new strength from the information revolution. And it is the type that we generally refer to in this study.

But there may also be hybrids of the three types, with different tasks being organized around different types of networks. For example, a networked actor may have an all-channel directorate at its core but use stars and chains for tactical operations. There may also be hybrids of network and hierarchical forms of organization. For example, traditional hierarchies may exist inside particular nodes in a network. Some actors may have a hierarchical organization overall but use network designs for tactical operations; other actors may have an all-channel design overall but use hierarchical teams for tactical operations. Many combinations and configurations are possible.

There is no established methodology to follow for analyzing networks, although the literature identifies many factors and attributes to consider. We examine the design and operation (or form and function) of a network—be it a chain, star, all-channel, or hybrid—in terms of four levels of analysis:

- Organizational level—To what extent is a set of actors organized as a network? What type of organization is it? This is the top level—a starting point—for assessing the extent to which a set of actors is designed for swarming. Among other things, assessment at this level, much of it discussed above, may include inquiring whether and how members may act autonomously, but also whether and how hierarchical dynamics that preclude autonomy may be mixed in with the network dynamics.

- Doctrinal level—Why have the members of an organization assumed a network form? Is it deliberate? What doctrines, interests, and other reasons or motivations exist for using and remaining in this form? This level of analysis is important for explaining what keeps a network together and enables the members to operate strategically and tactically, without necessarily having to resort to a central command or leader. The performance of the all-channel design in particular may depend on the existence of shared principles and practices that span all nodes and to which the members subscribe in a deep way. Such a set of principles—a doctrine—can enable them to be "all of one mind" even though they are dispersed and devoted to different tasks. It can provide the central ideational, strategic, and operational coherence that allows for tactical decentralization.

- Technological level—What is the pattern of, and the capacity for, dense information and communications flows? What technologies support this? How well do these technologies suit the organizational design? This level may involve a mix of new and old, high- and low-tech capabilities; but in general it is the new technologies that are making the new forms of organization and doctrine feasible. The higher the bandwidth, and the more advanced the means of transmission, reception, storage and retrieval, the better the prospects for network-style communications and organization. Design elements and capabilities at this level may significantly affect the organizational and doctrinal levels. The all-channel design in particular depends on the network having a capacity—indeed, a well-developed infrastructure—for the dense communication of functional information. This does not mean that all nodes must be in constant communication; that may not make sense. But when communication is needed, the network's members must be able to disseminate information as promptly and widely as desired within the network and to outside audiences.

• Social level—How well, and in what ways, are the members personally known and connected to each other? This is the classic level of social network analysis, where strong personal ties, often ones that rest on close friendship or bonding experiences, ensure high degrees of personal trust and loyalty. To function well, networks seem to require higher degrees of interpersonal trust than do other forms of organization, like hierarchies. This traditional level remains important in the information age.

The strength of a network, perhaps especially of the all-channel design, depends on functioning well across all four levels. The strongest networks will be those in which the organizational level is supported by a well-defined doctrine attuned to the overall design, and in which all this is layered atop advanced communications systems and rests on strong personal and social ties at the base. Each level, and the overall design, may benefit from redundancy and diversity. Each level's characteristics are thus likely to affect the other levels.

These are not idle academic issues. Swarm forces will have to be networked—and getting the network form right is a crucial enterprise. There may well be various design options that will merit consideration—and the assessment of these options should make sure that all the organizational, doctrinal, technological, and social levels are well-designed and integrated.

For example, a concept related to swarming, namely "network-centric warfare," rests on an important doctrinal notion: Victory in future battles will depend more on who has the best "networks" than on who has the strongest "platforms." But so far, writings about this concept have focused mainly on the technological level—on the information and communications "grids" that could enable the concept. It is far from clear how forces would actually be organized and deployed under this concept, and what would be the role and shape of network designs that may figure from the command down to the field level.

Envisioning Pods and Clusters

- **Comparative analysis: homogeneity, heterogeneity**
  - **Like-looking units with like functions, or**
  - **Mixed units, all having same mix of capabilities, or**
  - **Total heterogeneity, differing functions**
- **Size, scale, organizational issues**
  - **Platoon-sized pod, light-strike vehicle-mounted**
  - **Three pods a "cluster"—some direct firepower**
  - **Clusters capable of engaging battalions (e.g., ten clusters could defeat an enemy division)**
- ➜ **Pods, clusters amenable to aggregation in various ways, tailored to terrain, opponent, mission**

As one considers the possibility of creating military "pods" and "clusters" for a swarming force, a key question—beyond how big or small the pods and clusters should be—is what they should look like. There are, logically, several major alternatives. Pods may be homogeneous—i.e., like-looking, with all soldiers armed in like fashion, functioning in like ways. Or pods might be like-looking from one to the next, but each could have a mixed set of internal functions—e.g., combining a bombardment element, an antitank capability, and an infantry assault force. The last logical possibility embraces heterogeneity: Each pod would have a single function, but functions would differ across the cluster of pods—e.g., there would be an antitank pod, an air defense pod, and an assault pod, all in the same cluster.

While it is far too early to determine the optimal composition of pods and clusters, it is possible to note some trade-offs that might arise in selecting any of the above forms. For example, the option of crafting units in complete conformity with each other ensures that all pods can be counted on to be able to perform with comparable effectiveness—which may be a crucial factor in successful swarming. However, although this may make sense for strike pods, such an approach might be very vulnerable to factors like a loss of friendly air superiority. Mixed pods, all configured in like ways, might mitigate this risk—since they would all be likely to have organic strike, air defense, and antitank capabilities. Yet deciding to include significant self-defense capability in the pods waters down their offensive swarming punch. A last possibility would be to specialize the pods and clusters, so that a pod whose principal function is ground assault might be protected against tanks by another pod, and from air attack by yet another. The risk of specialization, of course, is that the likely wide dispersion of pods across the battlespace would result, perhaps quite often, in the pods being too far apart to provide adequate support to each other on a "just-in-time" basis. Clearly, this issue demands further conceptualizing.

How big should pods be? Since the pod is the suggested elemental force in ground force swarms, we suggest beginning with the most basic military unit: the platoon of roughly 40–45 soldiers, with ten light strike vehicles per pod. Since there appears to be no compelling reason to eschew the military penchant for groups of three, three pods would then form a cluster—which would itself be about one-half the size of existing U.S. Army companies. Thus, these new formations, with new functions, would still require about as much manpower as existing platoon-level formations, and not too much less than companies. Where our concepts begin to differ sharply from those that sustain the existing panoply of military formations is above the level of the cluster. Simply put, under a swarming doctrine there would be little need for the existing array of battalions, regiments, brigades, divisions, or corps. These forms of organization are designed for delivering and sustaining mass on linear battlefields. Swarming is about creating pulsed masses of fire and force at chosen moments, not continuously. The basic deployment of the swarms should be a wide dispersal—a fundamental doctrinal concept that runs counter to massing.

In this view, swarming pods organized into networked clusters, with an ability to engage from all directions simultaneously, could reasonably be expected to defeat a battalion-sized opponent (i.e., a 750–900 man force) operating along traditional lines.[40] Since a cluster may use as little as one-sixth the manpower of a battalion, it follows that a group of ten clusters ought to be able to defeat a division-sized adversary.[41] Of course, estimation has to be very rough at this point, because much analysis and experimentation is needed to flesh out an exact estimate of the potential military effectiveness of pods and clusters. Sensitivity analysis should be done for different types of pod compositions, with and without the effects of air superiority factored into the mix of variables. The efficacy of swarming may vary, depending upon terrain, or whether one is attacking or defending. Finally, sensitivity analysis of dispersed swarming formations must consider care-

---

[40]This is based on the assumption of the cluster having 30 light strike vehicles with crews capable of dismounted combat—all able to engage the enemy simultaneously. The power of the cluster comes from this kind of networking, where all engage all the time.

[41]Assuming an enemy armored division possesses from 250 to 300 tanks and an equal number of personnel carriers and other transports, our basic metric is that one light strike vehicle in a swarming force will have combat power equal to one tank. Since there are 300 strike vehicles in ten clusters, we hypothesize that a swarming force of this size will be able to take on a traditional armored division on at least equal terms. And this is *without* factoring in the effects of ground support aircraft and missile fire with guided submunitions.

fully the threat posed by a heavy, massed mechanized force—to answer the question about whether this is likely to be a great peril to the swarm force, or if it is actually the desired disposition of a massed enemy now susceptible to being decimated by swarmed fire.

A point to bear in mind is that pods and clusters may be aggregated in the battlespace in a wide variety of ways, depending upon variations in the terrain, the quality of the opponent, and the particular sort of mission that is being undertaken. Further, their dispersed deployment and high mobility will allow them to use the tactical defensive to their advantage, drawing enemy forces repeatedly into "kill zones." And if the notion of eliminating many existing military organizational forms seems too radical, perhaps it will help to remember that the remarkable Roman legions were built almost entirely upon "centuries" of about 100 men each.

The battalion formation itself did not come along until the 16th century, nor did the division until the 18th century (Keegan, 1993; Black, 1994). As a dominant form of organization, the corps came into its own—disastrously—in World War I. Since the end of that war (1918), there has been a steady trend away from massed ground formations. World War II initially featured divisions instead of corps; but, even in that conflict, smaller *kampfgruppen* and combat commands came to dominate. Indeed, the combined arms *kampfgruppe* that emerged in the early days of the blitzkrieg (see Guderian, 1957) may prove to be the best transitional model that can be employed in a move beyond AirLand Battle to what we call a BattleSwarm doctrine.

As the Tofflers have put it (1993), the trend in the 20th century has been toward "demassification." Even though the Gulf War seems an exception to this trend, it much more likely represents, in our view, a last, loving look at mass-based warfare—a last look before the rise of swarming.

The organizational change that we are calling for—keeping but retooling the most basic existing military forms—is similar to the corporate redesign principle of "flattening," that often features the removal of middle layers of management. This has proven successful in the ongoing revolution in business affairs and may prove equally useful in the military realm.

Connectivity and Control

- **Connectivity essential**
  - **Too little restricts adaptability—but too much creates perturbations**
  - **Enduring tension: decontrol v. micromanagement**
- **Internetting and swarming**
  - **Internetting highly advisable—can serve doctrines besides swarming**
  - **Swarming requires internetting—a type of network-centric warfare**

If a military doctrine based on swarming pods and clusters is to arise, its emergence will surely depend upon developing new approaches to connectivity and control, and achieving a new balance between the two. A key issue is likely to be how to deal with the tension between the benefits of broad connectivity, and the risks that too much of a good thing could create unintended perturbations in field operations, leading to a loss of control. Clearly, the greater the connectivity, the higher the "average engagement level" of the many pod and cluster formations in the field. But it must also be recognized that, under conditions approaching all-channel connectivity, groups of pods and clusters that lack topsight face some risk of devoting their efforts to targets of lesser importance. Further, full connectivity, improperly utilized, might actually foster indecision, with pods and clusters growing uncertain about how to focus their efforts from one moment to the next. After all, Clausewitz's "friction" may be greater than ever on a nonlinear battle-space. Perhaps worse, forces may be subject to disorganizing "entropy" more than slowing friction. However, proper connectivity, properly used, can mitigate all of these problems, enabling skillful leaders and their troops to find their way amid the confusion.

These problems are reminiscent of the dilemma of d'Erlon's corps at Waterloo, which spent nearly the whole first day of the battle wandering back and forth between the engagement with the British at Quatre Bras and the engagement with the Prussians at

Ligny—never joining in either fight. D'Erlon's problem, largely, was that he actually had too much information—of a conflicting variety—to choose decisively one action over another. Napoleon himself complicated matters further by sending a stream of self-contradictory orders that kept d'Erlon hopping between the two battles. As David Chandler (1966, p. 1052) has put it,

> d'Erlon's command spent the entire afternoon and evening marching and countermarching between the two fields of battle without firing a shot at either; and the full irony of the situation was, of course, that the Ist Corps' effective intervention on either scene of action would have resulted in a major French victory.

D'Erlon's dilemma highlights, to a degree, the enduring need to avoid either full decontrol or intensive micromanagement.

Appropriate improvements in connectivity may, of course, prove an unalloyed benefit even if the current, mass-based military doctrine is preserved well into the future. Better information operations could give our standing AirLand Battle doctrine new "legs." But even though better connectivity can improve doctrines other than swarming, swarming would optimize the benefits wrought by good connectivity. Swarming should allow more units of maneuver to engage more of the time, in more efficient ways. In this respect, swarming may be a way to actualize the potential of the Navy's emerging doctrine of "network-centric warfare"—which seeks, through improvements in connectivity and decontrol, to enhance the effectiveness of naval strike forces (see Cebrowski and Garstka, 1998).

The technological requirements for achieving high levels of connectivity are daunting. But, if we are to move to a swarm doctrine—one we term "BattleSwarm"—these obstacles will have to be surmounted.

Technological Requirements Onerous

- **Key challenges for moving to a BattleSwarm doctrine**
  - **Advances in information structuring, processing**
  - **Pod, clusters need robustness against disruption**
- **Enabling technologies exist, requirements onerous**
  - **Dense communication of functional information**
  - **Mobile "mesh nets" now technologically feasible**
  - **All-channel network as key form of organization**
- **Digital communications empower swarm networks**
  - **All components can engage much of the time**
  - **A force multiplier of small force**

The technological requirements for designing swarming forces and moving to a swarming doctrine will surely be onerous. In this study, we can do no more than briefly highlight and sketch a handful of them.

If swarming is to take hold as the next major military doctrine under a concept like BattleSwarm (see next chapter), two information-driven challenges will have to be surmounted. First, serious advances are required in the management of information. This refers both to improving the speed of processing, but also to learning to structure flows and stocks of information more usefully. In our view, the information structuring challenge is the more difficult one—it goes to the heart of the matter of how to winnow important information from nonessential; and to the issue of who will know what during battle.

A second challenge is not about managing one's own information; rather, it is about protecting one's flows against disruption by the enemy. The robustness of the communications networks that undergird and enable the operations of pods and clusters in the field must be ensured against all manner of disruption. Of particular concern in this area are electronic warfare, generally, and pulse-generating weapons systems in particular. This problem is crucially important because swarm forces depend upon uninterrupted flows of information to actualize their potential. Disruption of these flows will not only render pods and clusters less effective, but can also make them vulnerable to being "picked off" in detail—one by one.

Enabling technologies already exist that can meet the onerous informational requirements that swarming will impose. In almost all cases, commercial-off-the-shelf (COTS) technology is available that can support a swarm's need for the dense communication of time-urgent functional information. The networking capabilities of a number of software programs also suggest that properly configured mobile "mesh nets" are also now technologically feasible. Finally, it is also clear that all-channel interconnectivity is available. Whether it is universally desirable is a different issue, and one worth exploring. In our view, experiments should be undertaken with varying degrees of connectivity, with all-channel networks perhaps limited to specific tactical areas of operations. The risk, if limits are not imposed on connectivity, is one of fostering "clogged circuits" or other drags on operating efficiency.

Clearly, digital communications enable the rise of swarm networks. They provide for smooth cascades of information and for the level of information security that will be needed in an increasingly dispersed, nonlinear battlespace of the future. The consequence of poor information security will be high for a swarm force if it becomes compromised—but then the cost of intercepted and decoded communications has always been high. In 207 B.C., during the later years of the Second Punic War, a Carthaginian messenger was caught by the Romans, leading to the deadly ambush of Hasdrubal's army at the Metaurus—and to the overall defeat of Carthage (Creasy, 1851, pp. 84–110). Two millennia later, at the Battle of Tannenberg in the opening month of World War I, German radio intercepts of Russian field movements allowed an outnumbered force under Hindenburg to win a signal victory that tipped the scales much in Germany's favor.[42]

Robust communications that help with both the structuring and processing of information will enable most pods and clusters to engage the enemy most of the time—a key aspect of swarming. If this can be done consistently, it holds out the possibility of creating a new kind of force-multiplying effect, whereby a skillful blending of the technological and organizational aspects of information operations can enable a relatively small force to outperform an ostensibly larger one.

---

[42]Keegan (1998, pp. 147–148) also points out that the Germans had just as lax an information security regime—both sides suffered from shortages in code books, operators, and translators. Yet, it was the Russians who suffered when the German commander, Hindenburg, "was passed the transcript of a complete Russian First Army order for an advance to the siege of Königsberg."

Information Operations Enable Swarming

- **Information operations key to military operations**
  - **More than just an exotic, or specialty function**
  - **Part of overall environment of conflict**
- **"Information dominance" has a dual purpose**
  - **Damage enemy information flows**
  - **Protect one's own information assets**

From the foregoing discussion, it should be clear that information operations are central to future military operations, writ large. Information operations should be viewed, not as an exotic or specialty function, but rather as an integral part of the overall emerging doctrinal environment.

Actually, this has been the case for successful militaries throughout history, with regard to the information operations of their day. For example, the sweep of the Mongol conquests was largely a function of the speed with which the Arrow Riders conveyed information and of the willingness of the khans to decontrol their (often outnumbered) "hordes" operationally and tactically (see Chambers, 1985; Curtin, 1908). Similarly, the Pax Britannica brought about by the Royal Navy was due to its superiority in battle—which owed much to advances made in signaling, most notably the Hopham flag-hoist system. But the greatest British naval successes were achieved when swift information processing (and structuring, in the case of the Hopham system) was wedded to a willingness to diverge from the rigid doctrinal controls of the "fighting instructions," allowing ship captains much more leeway for improvised, but still coordinated, actions—the essence of Nelson's notion of his subordinates being a "band of brothers" (Mahan, 1898). The British case—and that of the Mongols—reflects the integral role that information operations should have in formulating and executing advanced military doctrines.

For swarming to work, these lessons about information operations forming a key part of the overall environment of conflict will have to be absorbed. If information is viewed as a "niche" product, rather than something that enlivens and energizes *all* operations, then it will be unlikely that the great potential of "information dominance" (Arquilla, 1994) will be actualized. This term does not mean knowing everything that can be known; rather, it means knowing sufficiently more than the adversary, enough to achieve decisive effects during a conflict. Thus, information dominance is a relative rather than an absolute concept.

The process of gaining and exploiting information dominance has two fundamental aspects. The first—the one that is generally emphasized—is about the things that can be done *to* an adversary to disrupt his information flows. This is most often thought of as electronic attacks on command and control structures. But it may also include physical destruction of key communications nodes and damage to the *contents* of the enemy's information resources, not just to the conduits of his information flows. Under this broader notion of the types of damage to be inflicted, deception and psychological operations may become prominently featured in the mix of tools to be used.

The second core element in information operations relates to managing the stocks and flows, the contents and conduits, of one's own informational resources. This is a generally less emphasized aspect of information operations—but is likely to be of great importance to the success of swarming as a doctrine. For a swarming field operation to succeed, the units of maneuver must be able to rely on uninterrupted flows of useful information—i.e., both information processing and structuring must be assured. This may enable the swarming force to prevail even against an adversary whose own information flows are not disrupted; because the swarm will still be able to target the enemy, pulse to the attack, dissever, and then recombine for continued assaults. Of course, disrupting the enemy's communications is an added bonus and should be attempted. But more weight can and should be put upon the information management function.[43] This emphasis will, in turn, reinforce the networked organizational structures and practices of the swarm.

Our concern about the primacy of managing one's own information resources implies a need to analyze closely the sensitivity of swarming to disruption of the swarm's information flows. The next section surveys ways in which swarming might be undermined or countered—and finds that there are a wide variety of means for attacking the communications-driven core of the notion of swarming.

---

[43]This was also true of blitzkrieg: The Germans put two-way radios in all their panzers, giving their tankers more information and enabling the close coordination that became the hallmark of modern armored operations (see Mellenthin, 1956).

Must Reduce Technical Vulnerabilities of Communications

- **Defending information flows a paramount goal**
- **Yet internetted swarm vulnerable to pulse weapons**
  - **High-altitude nuclear detonation (HEMP)**
  - **High-power microwave weapons (HPM)**
- **Risks of conventional physical destruction**
- **Radio frequency bombs and grenades**
- **Risks of corruption of data, or exploitation by enemy**

Swarming clearly depends—far more than traditional approaches to battle—upon robust information flows as much as it does upon the proper structuring of data for operational use by networked units. Securing these flows, therefore, can be seen as a necessary condition for successful swarming. However, meeting this condition is likely to prove a stern challenge. There are numerous ways in which the information flow may be disrupted—from classic electronic jamming to more sophisticated forms of computer network attack. However, few current or potential adversaries have these means at hand. This may encourage them to return to thinking about the utility of nuclear weapons, both on the battlefield—to offset the American revolution in military affairs— and above it, to disrupt communications.

One of the most effective means of breaking down communications is by an airburst of a nuclear weapon at a high altitude. This generation of a highly disruptive electromagnetic pulse (EMP) would temporarily disable most communications in the battlespace; it would also damage the many embedded information systems that make modern weapons systems able to fire with accuracy (e.g., the optical sights of a main battle tank). The fact that the EMP is generated by a nuclear detonation—against which there are strong normative inhibitions—suggests that there are few actors who might actually be able to undertake such an action. Yet, we note the frequent discussion of EMP as a likely threat in cold war–era ruminations on nuclear strategy.[44] Further, the high-altitude nature of the burst means that there would be virtually no collateral damage. Finally, it should be noted that the Russian military's declaratory stance with respect to nuclear weapons has moved, in recent years, from "no first use" to a willingness to engage in "first use." It may be that their inability to match American advances in conventional warfighting will impel the Russians to try to make up for any deficiencies in this manner. Indeed, the recently announced new Russian military doctrine is clearly more permissive of the use of nuclear weapons, from the tactical to the strategic level.

Along more exotic lines, information flows may come to be attacked in the future by high-power microwave weapons, which work on the basis of transforming the kinetic energy of electrons into a disruptive microwave field (see Benford, 1998). Additionally, several other sorts of directed energy and radio frequency weapons are beginning to appear, each of which may be able, eventually, to pose serious threats to information flows. Today, these weapons all suffer from two major problems: limited effective range and an inability to reduce their weaponized size down to the level at which they would be useful on the battlefield. These difficulties suggest, then, a growing emphasis by adversaries on finding cyberspace-based means for corrupting data, or slowing or stopping critical information flows. To date, though, this means of attack seems more useful for purposes of gaining access to sensitive information than in taking down systems— with the notable exception of the disruption done by the "Red team" in the "Eligible Receiver" exercise.

In addition to the innovative use of nuclear weapons for disrupting flows of information, and of other exotics and cyberspace-based means, there is also the possibility of using conventional weapons against key information nodes. This probably means achieving disruption by means of aerial bombardment, including missile barrages, since only this mode of attack seems to have a clear, conventional potential for achieving the level of disruption needed to head off the kind of swarming operations that we envision. However, it might also be theoretically possible to approximate such a campaign through the use of special forces engaging in "cybotage." There are historical examples of both approaches being used in World War II. Before D-Day, for example, Allied air forces struck systematically at the 90 German radar stations on the western coasts of occupied France, Belgium, and Holland. This effort blinded the Germans—with the exception of some sites in the Pas de Calais that were deliberately left intact, as part of a deception scheme (Breuer, 1993)—and played a big role in slowing their response to the invasion. Several months later, during the Battle of the Bulge, the Germans used special forces, operating behind the lines, to disrupt information flows by a variety of means—and were initially quite successful.

---

[44]See especially the technical discussions in Gottfried and Blair (1988, pp. 111–120); and Glasstone and Dolan (1977).

In short, there are a multitude of ways in which the robust information flow that forms the basis of swarming may be threatened. Nuclear, conventional, and unconventional means may all pose serious threats to a swarming force. Indeed, a widely dispersed deployment of pods and clusters may be subject to defeat in detail if their communications are disrupted. Therefore, securing information flows must be viewed as a key aspect of information operations.

Technical Vulnerabilities, cont.

- **Technological remedies can help, but would cost**
  - **Hardening of communications possible—but would undermine COTS benefits**
  - **Shielding and redundancy should be explored**
- **Nontechnological fixes worth trying**
  - **Raise political cost of nuclear HEMP**
  - **Train forces in "fighting blind"**
  - **Develop fallback doctrines for field units**

Basically, the means for mitigating this exposure fall into two categories: technical and nontechnical remedies. On the technical side, the clearest solution lies in hardening communications. But this runs up against the problem of undermining the economic and efficiency benefits of the wide use of COTS technologies. Hardening all communications would either require separate contracts for specific military use of such equipment or the retrofitting of COTS items. Either approach is likely to engender substantial costs. However, it may be possible to employ a technical fix that is less daunting: shielding. Basically, shielding would be a way to deal with nuclear EMP, HPM, and other radiofrequency and directed-energy weapons. It would consist principally of keeping communications equipment in lead boxes as much of the time as possible. In a full-blown swarming battle, however, this would likely prove too constraining. So, in addition to shielding, enhanced redundancy—such as carrying extra communications equipment in lead-lined boxes—may be advisable as an additional remedy.

Beyond technical fixes, though, a strategy of political and doctrinal initiatives could further shore up the information security needs of the swarm. For example, high-level policymakers could articulate that *any* nuclear detonation—even at high altitude—will be treated as a nuclear attack, inviting and allowing U.S. retaliation. Thus, we may be able to deter one of the major threats to the information flows of swarming forces.[45] Another solution might be found at the doctrinal level, including the explicit development of a doctrine for "fighting blind"—as a very last resort. In the case of swarming forces, this doctrine might entail moving to prearranged positions or just shifting to the tactical defensive. For the Royal Navy in the Napoleonic era, a ship that lost touch with its command during a battle was expected to follow the "fighting instructions'" injunction to "fall back on the Channel." Doctrinal remedies have long been around and have long provided important hedges against the failures of critical systems.

This section has outlined a variety of threats to the U.S. military's ability to move toward swarming. There are indeed many vulnerabilities. But, there are also a variety of available fixes, both technical and nontechnical in nature. In particular, a program could be undertaken to mitigate these exposures via hardening and redundancy. Although costlier than relying on COTS communications systems, hardening and redundancy appear in our analysis to be among the best available protections against these threats.

We cannot pretend to have said the final word on this issue; but we do believe that we have outlined a strategic approach to dealing effectively with the threats likely to be posed to the communications of swarming forces. For us, this is enough at present to warrant further analysis of our notion of the BattleSwarm and how to build one—topics that we discuss in the next chapter.

---

[45]Needless to say, such a position would also shore up our communications in pursuit of an AirLand Battle campaign as well. For a thoughtful, wide-ranging analysis of these issues, see Edwards (1997, pp. 61–80). However, the threat of nuclear retaliation in response to a high-altitude nuclear burst may have little credibility with a desperate opponent and may engender very high political costs of its own. This suggests that holding open the option to respond in a nuclear fashion should be viewed with much skepticism; and, if adopted, ought to be greatly complemented by hardening, shielding, and redundancy-based and doctrinal solutions. Indeed, reliance upon these latter techniques might even obviate the need to consider nuclear responses.

Chapter Five

TOWARD A "BATTLESWARM" DOCTRINE

From AirLand Battle . . .

- **AirLand Battle as zenith of maneuver warfare**
  - **Best tradition of air-ground jointness**
  - **Favors large formations (armored divisions)**
  - **Little or no naval involvement**
- **Limitations of AirLand Battle**
  - **Large formations increasingly vulnerable**
  - **Costly to maintain such forces**
  - **Useful mainly at high end of spectrum**

In Germany's stunning victories in the Battle of France in 1940 and early in the campaign in Russia in 1941, the German armed forces showed the world the great potential of a new military doctrine—blitzkrieg—based on the cooperation of tank and plane. Fifty years later, U.S. armed forces won a similarly impressive ground-air campaign against Iraq, utilizing an "AirLand Battle" doctrine that has clear roots in blitzkrieg. In this respect, the American victory in the Gulf[46] should be seen as the zenith of 20th century maneuver warfare, a style of battle that strongly favors large armored formations and relies on naval power almost solely to provide strategic "lift."[47]

The lop-sided victory over Saddam Hussein has sparked much discussion of it as representing a decisive "turning point"—perhaps a revolution—in military affairs (e.g., see

---

[46]Although the coalition against Iraq numbered over two dozen nations, U.S. forces provided the bulk of troops, aircraft, and naval assets. The victory must thus be seen as a triumph of American arms. For the seminal document elucidating the AirLand Battle doctrine, see *U.S. Army Field Manual 100-5*.

[47]In the Gulf War, the U.S. Navy did provide some shore bombardment, with weapons ranging from battleship guns to carrier strike aircraft and Tomahawk missiles. But these had little to do with the "left hook" armored maneuver that outflanked the Iraqi army in Kuwait. See Freedman and Karsh (1993). However, the Navy did play a role in pinning down Iraqis to the Gulf coast, in anticipation of an invasion that never came—a successful deception that diverted eight to ten Iraqi divisions. On this, see Friedman (1991, pp. 229–232).

Ederington and Mazarr, 1994; and Toffler and Toffler, 1993). But, while it is indisputable that the AirLand Battle doctrine was executed well in the Gulf, too much can be read into the outcome of this conflict. After all, the Iraqis faced a large coalition that had complete air and naval mastery—and information dominance to boot. This was not a particularly tough test of U.S. military doctrine. Indeed, our very success exposed some limitations of AirLand Battle that will likely make it less useful in the coming years.

First, the tremendous accuracy of precision-guided munitions (PGM)—at the tactical and strategic levels—suggests that large military formations, and the logistics on which they depend, are becoming increasingly vulnerable. What if the U.S. armored forces and close support aircraft come up against a PGM-rich adversary? We may still prevail; but large formations of armor and mechanized infantry will have a harder time. And this is very much part of a century-long trend toward dispersion on the battlefield—for example, the serried ranks of suicidal British infantry, advancing shoulder-to-shoulder at the Somme, were displaced by more spread-out formations in World War II. Greater dispersion should be expected now that the information content of weapons has almost severed the age-old link between range and accuracy.

Another concern should be about the massive nature of an American field army going about the business of AirLand Battle. This is a very costly sort of enterprise and grows more so all the time. Aside from the natural growth in the costs of manpower and materials, there is an increasing need to spend more on protecting the tank. A great deal of research is being done to try to allow the main battle tank to survive hits by precision-guided munitions, with the major focus today being on composite and explosive-reactive armor. In many ways, this resembles the earlier—and ultimately futile—effort to extend the useful life of the battleship by armoring it ever more heavily, so it might withstand more hits from air and long-range naval guns.[48] Current defense policy analysis should turn, instead, to considering what alternative force structures are possible for the same, or lower, cost—and what sorts of savings in deployment time may be accrued by the shift to an alternative approach.

Finally, it seems clear that AirLand Battle is a doctrine aimed at dominating the high end of the spectrum of conflict. Designed to guide the fight against a Russian invasion in Europe, it served well in the Gulf, where our opponent obligingly deployed a large field army on open, tankable terrain—and then allowed us several months for a stately buildup. Future conflicts are less likely to feature such permissive characteristics for AirLand Battle. It is therefore incumbent upon the U.S. military to consider doctrinal alternatives that better allow for operations across the spectrum of conflict—using the whole force, rather than just some specially trained subset of forces.

---

[48]Current experimentation with lighter vehicles does suggest, however, that the Army is beginning to shift its focus toward speed and maneuverability—a very positive sign.

If there is a way to move the *whole* force to a new, more flexible doctrine, then that should be explored, because this is likely to be a solution superior to one that deepens the sense of our having a "bifurcated army." The problem with trying to retain forces capable of waging an AirLand Battle while cultivating a BattleSwarm force is that we might spend ever more heavily and end up with a force incapable of conducting either form of war. Further, "heavy" forces will be increasingly vulnerable to precision-guided munitions, which are now diffusing throughout the world. In addition, the existing doctrinal approach is very limiting. In the Gulf War, the U.S. military enjoyed the benefit of being able to mass its forces for over six months prior to the start of ground operations. The fact that this kind of time was not available in Kosovo in the spring of 1999—but was needed to fight the kind of war we wanted—meant that the ground option was basically ruled out from the beginning in favor of an air war. A swarm force will be able to deal with time-space constraints on military action—which should prove salutary for deterrence and crisis stability in the future.

Swarming, we hypothesize, provides an important alternative vision of the future for the American military—and it may well do so for other militaries, too, if they begin looking for innovations that may enable them to outwit the Americans. Whoever gets there first may find in swarming the doctrinal catalyst for waging *cyberwar*—the military end of the information-age conflict spectrum that has long been a central theme in our research (see Arquilla and Ronfeldt, 1993).

. . . to BattleSwarm

- **Potential benefits of moving to BattleSwarm**
  - **Optimize networking potential afforded by IO**
  - **Join all services in operations**
  - **Apply across spectrum of conflict: HIC to LIC**
  - **Relate to nonmilitary agencies**
- **Benefits of smaller forces and dispersed units**
  - **Lower budgetary costs**
  - **Less (but more complex) logistical demands**
  - **Decreased vulnerability to enemy PGMs**

There are many reasons to identify and develop a new military doctrine now. A compelling one is that the evolution of information operations (IO) is now sufficiently advanced to assure the optimization of the network form of organization in battle. This means that more "shooters" could be engaged, more of the time, and that a higher level of engagement can be sustained throughout a campaign. Beyond this higher "utilization rate," the total pool of shooters grows, because the network in this sort of fighting may draw naval strike forces into the mix much more extensively than is the case with AirLand Battle. The full potential of joint operations is more likely to be realized by what we call BattleSwarm.

Another value of moving to a swarming doctrine is that it is likely to prove just as useful in low- as high-intensity conflict (LIC and HIC) settings and across all types of terrain. This should be the case mainly because striking the adversary from all directions—either with fire or in force—ought to work against either a massed or a dispersed opponent. And a true swarming force will have at its core the small pods and clusters capable of operating against foes of any size—combining to confront large field armies and aggregating far more loosely and distributively in operations aimed at countering guerrillas and other unconventional forces.

These same pods and clusters should also prove adept at handling the small-scale contingencies of the future, since they will be able to keep the peace by maintaining a swarming presence. The U.S. intervention in Haiti during the 1990s, for example, featured a good bit of swarming of this peaceful variety, with relatively small numbers of American forces "blanketing" the potential trouble spots throughout the country with their deterring presence. It is important to observe, in this case, that the U.S. forces operating in Haiti had overwhelming support of the local populace. Were the situation otherwise, the results of swarming in force may well have been problematic. Another benefit of the kind of presence a swarming force affords is that closer, better relations with humanitarian agencies and NGOs may be undertaken during an operation. A swarming force's smaller size should also generate less local resentment, making coordination with NGOs easier—while the pods and clusters will still have considerable "punch" at hand or on call.

As to the economics of swarming, it seems clear from our earlier analysis that a force based on small, light units will cost substantially less than the existing heavy force—which features nearly 2,000 tanks and a very complicated support structure designed to place and sustain them on the battlefield.[49] The dispersed, nonlinear concept of operations that guides BattleSwarm will require complex new logistical practices; but the smaller absolute size of the swarm force should reduce overall supply requirements, while at the same time giving the swarm force the ability to engage the enemy with a larger percentage of the overall field force than has been the case under existing and previous doctrines. This last point may prove to be the crucial "difference that makes a difference" about swarming—radically changing the patterns of attrition and allowing ever more to be achieved with smaller units.

Finally, field forces organized in pods and clusters will be far less vulnerable than are conventional armored or mechanized formations to the precision-guided munitions now diffusing to militaries throughout the world. Thus, shifting to swarming will solve the emerging problem of expensive, heavy forces being ever more vulnerable to cheap, highly accurate weapons. This concern has already motivated and guided some experiments, with interesting results.

---

[49]For the present, we do not call for radical changes in the composition of U.S. naval and air forces—we believe that their existing hardware, if properly organized in network fashion, can serve the supporting fire needs of the BattleSwarm. However, we note that the Navy is actually thinking about developing large numbers of small surface combatants—the so-called "street-fighter" concept (see Hughes, 2000). As to Army restructuring, a useful set of ruminations on the subject can be found in MacGregor (1997).

Promising Results of Recent Developments

- **Army After Next (AAN)—selective advances**
- **Hunter Warrior (USMC)—comprehensive changes**
- **Force XXI (USA)—new technology, old organization**
- **Fleet Battle Experiment Bravo (USN)—old tech, new org**
- **Air Expeditionary Forces (USAF)—composite changes**
- **Urban Swarm (USMC)—*avant garde* initiative**
- ✔ **Advisable future agenda items**
  - **Shift focus to coevolution of technological, organizational, and doctrinal changes**
  - **Experiment with notions of pods and clusters**

Moving to a BattleSwarm approach for military operations would be a radical departure from the way things are, but it may be easier than it appears. Each of the services has been engaged in a series of doctrinal and organizational, not to mention technical, experiments whose results are generally quite promising and may point the way to developing and adopting a swarming doctrine. Future military contingencies will require the U.S. military to develop the means to deploy to and fight in distant theaters much more quickly than the current organizational structures allow. This may well result in an increased "demand" for lighter, swifter, yet just-as-effective applications of force. From all the experimentation going on, it seems clear that senior military leadership is well aware of this growing need.

A number of advanced conceptual initiatives are under way. One led by the Army is its "Army After Next" (AAN) program. Encouraged by the Training and Doctrine Command (TRADOC), substantial analytic work has commenced largely around the notion of empowering light forces to be able to take on a much heavier (armored) opposition. Most of the work thus far has been conceptual, supplemented with sophisticated simulations of battle settings (e.g., see Matsumura et al., 1999).[50] The findings to date suggest that light forces, if well-informed and armed with standoff guided weapons,[51] can indeed perform capably against heavy adversaries. These latest findings somewhat revise earlier, more skeptical views on the subject (e.g., see Steeb et al., 1996). The latest work even includes some organizational change, in that seven-man squads are aggregated—in succeeding multiples of six—into larger "elements" and "units."

While similar to our "pods" and their parent "clusters," these elements and units have thus far been considered only in terms of their potential for defensive tasks (Matsumura et al., 1999, p. 19). In our view, a swarming doctrine would not only make light battle units into better defenders, but would also improve their offensive capabilities. Clearly, this further doctrinal dimension should be worth adding to this promising research. To some extent, the U.S. Marine Corps is already doing this in its Hunter Warrior/Sea Dragon advanced war-fighting experiments. These share the AAN's technical and organizational advances but add the objective of giving such a force an offensive punch.

In this regard, the Marine field experiments have clearly gone beyond their Army counterpart, known as the Army Force XXI, or Experimental Force. The Army's focus on examining the impact of new technologies has generally overlooked how best to go about wedding them to new organizational forms. Interestingly, the reverse seems the case in the Navy "Fleet Battle" experiments, where older technologies are being enlivened by experimenting with new organizational forms based on Vice Admiral Cebrowski's (1998) concept of "network-centric warfare."

Meanwhile, the latest Air Force and Marine experiments involve sophisticated efforts to blend technological, organizational, and doctrinal innovations. The United States Air Force, for example, has pioneered an "air expeditionary force" notion that pulls all the elements together. Air wings, for example, may be of shifting or highly mixed composition—i.e., the "composite wing," in which fighters and bombers, and other aircraft types may be closely joined, specifically tailored to the needs of particular theaters or missions. At the doctrinal level, the Air Force has long been habituated—by the very sense of its ability to reach far and wide—to thinking about the battlespace in large, nonlinear terms. The Marines also exhibit virtually all these elements, as showcased in avant garde concepts like Urban Warrior/Swarm, where very small units, known as "infestation teams," get to operate in a highly decentralized but extensively internetted fashion. The very latest Marine Corps field experiments have explicitly adopted the concept of "Chechen swarming"—in apparent recognition of the highly effective Chechen use of small units in omnidirectional attacks against a classically configured military (on this, see Arquilla and Karasik, 1999, and Fuentes, 2000).

---

[50]However, field work is under way with two Army brigades at Fort Lewis, Washington, where a concerted effort is exploring—mostly in technological terms—the potential for a small, light battle force that could be used for rapid deployment in various crises. See Edward Offley, "Fast Strike Force Being Developed at Fort Lewis," *The Seattle Post Intelligencer,* November 3, 1999.

[51]Along with networked air and naval fire support.

These developments should be cause for some celebration and also encourage some next steps. Two are needed soon. First, there should be a shift to conceptual and experimental work that will integrate more explicitly all the technological, organizational, and doctrinal elements of change that are in play. Military advances have, in almost all cases, featured the coevolution of these factors (blitzkrieg, with its tank, plane, and panzer division being a case in point). Second, to incorporate fully the organizational and doctrinal possibilities of the latest in advanced weaponry and communications systems, it is time to begin a process of experimenting with pods and clusters—using them in a swarming fashion under demanding conditions. Let it be shown whether these small units, and the swarming concept itself, can do well. Skepticism aside, there is a demonstrated need to try such experiments—especially given the interesting work on the AAN and on the Marine infestation teams.[52]

Finally, there is another reason to begin coevolutionary experiments using pods and clusters (or otherwise-named small units)—there is already proof of their utility. In Battle Command Training Program (BCTP) simulation exercises during the first months of 1994, the 7th Special Forces Group attached itself to the XVIII Airborne Corps in wargames aimed at figuring out how to defend Saudi Arabia with light forces. Initial exercises went poorly, overall, for the light force—which often held up the invaders but always incurred very heavy casualties. In this first phase, the special forces were used almost exclusively for reconnaissance—as was the case during Desert Shield/Storm, along with coalition support. But at one point, the commander of the special forces asked that his small, dispersed units be given strike designation tasks as well. The results were both immediate and astonishing: The special forces became the enablers of highly effective swarming of fire. Heavily armored invaders were routinely defeated—and XVIII Corps casualties plummeted, on average, by over 80 percent (Phillips, 1995). The conditions underlying this unexpected success must be replicated and systematically examined.

---

[52]The Marine Corps has been moving in innovative directions for years now—even before the rise of its "infestation teams" and "Chechen swarms." For example, see *Fleet Marine Force Manual 6*, "Ground Combat Operations" (1995).

BattleSwarm vis à vis Other Concepts for Exploiting America's "Information Edge"

- **"Convergent assault"**
  - **Relies heavily on heliborne mobility**
  - **Aims for simultaneous, omnidirectional attacks**
- **"Nodal warfare"**
  - **Striking at key "nodes"—a network-like concept**
  - **Swarming may be both nodal and nodeless**
- **"Network-centric warfare"**
  - **Views battlespace as "networks" with "grids"**
  - **Swarming a type of NCW**
- **"System of systems" and "cooperative weapon systems"**
  - **Sees massive, complex, C4ISR-led connections**
  - **Swarming benefits—so do other paradigms**

Parts of the U.S. military are already awash in doctrinal ferment as various new concepts are being considered for exploiting America's "information edge." Swarming—specifically, BattleSwarm—may provide a comprehensive concept of operations that can catalyze and integrate these many strands of new thinking.

Consider, for example, notions of a nearly tank-less type of "convergent assault" (Coroalles, 1991) that relies heavily on helicopters for tactical mobility. It offers a way to engage in simultaneous, omnidirectional attacks upon heavier adversary forces. Swarming, particularly the idea of "pulsing" to the attack, may become an even better conceptual framework for the whole notion of "convergence" by light, heliborne forces. Of course, the larger challenge for this concept is the inherent vulnerability of helicopters—a cause of serious problems for earlier, "rotor-based" doctrines during the Vietnam era (e.g., the Marines' "vertical envelopment" and the Army's "air assault").

Another important advanced concept is "nodal warfare," a nascent doctrine based on the notion of striking at key enemy pressure points (especially command and control nodes). This approach is inherently network-oriented and is consistent with the thoughts of many airpower theorists, old and new (e.g., see Mitchell, [1928] 1960; DeSeversky, 1942; and Warden, 1988). More recently, Admiral William Owens (1995) has articulated an explicit exposition of "nodal warfare." This concept is attractive, because it has the potential to take on a network-oriented slant, despite its seeming drift toward a more centralized approach. A swarming doctrine could enliven this concept further. However, a swarming doctrine should guide campaigns not only against key nodes, but also against adversaries who may be essentially "nodeless" (i.e., operating autonomously or semiautonomously, like some guerrilla, terrorist, or other irregular forces).

Vice Admiral Cebrowski's (1998) concept of "network-centric warfare" (NCW) is another important idea that may be enlivened by swarming. Unlike Owens' nodal notions, which are focused on the adversary, Cebrowski's views have more to do with how one's own forces may network themselves to take full advantage of new approaches to the structuring and processing of information flows. His idea of "grids," overlaid across the battlespace, may provide inspiration for the application of swarming tactics—swarming may be seen as a natural fit to network-centric warfare.

Owens (1995) also has ideas about improving the structuring and processing of one's own informational capabilities and resources, neatly exposited in his concept of the "system of systems," and in its corollary, the idea of "cooperative weapon systems." These notions take networking to its logical terminus—a place where massive, complex, C4ISR-led interconnections shape the contours of the military campaign. Such a system, of course, could greatly increase opportunities for engaging in swarming—but if used in centralizing fashion, would benefit AirLand Battle, too, it should be noted.

What can be seen from our review of these other leading-edge concepts is that the BattleSwarm concept plays a role in all of them. Swarming could become the guiding principle behind "convergent assault" and "nodal warfare"—and could enliven the field experiments with some of the concepts going on currently at Fort Lewis. Further, the notions of "network-centric warfare" and the emerging "system of systems" have the opportunity to make effective swarming possible. In short, swarming may be viewed as both an enabler and a beneficiary of the most advanced warfighting concepts currently being fielded. This suggests a need to move ahead with further development of the BattleSwarm doctrine.

The Challenge Ahead

- Primary challenges are organizational
    - More and deeper jointness than ever before
    - Greatly decentralized command authority
    - Skillful information resource management
    - Guarded data sharing with semitrusted allies

- Technological hurdles also loom large
    - Internetted communications—hardened, redundant
    - Tools for decoying and deceiving enemy
    - Interoperability in combined operations crucial

Ω This "interwar period" ideal for moving to BattleSwarm

Suppose that BattleSwarm—a doctrine that envisages swarming formations based on the dispersed deployment and robust internetting of myriad, mostly small units of maneuver, some dedicated to close-in combat and others to distant fire—were deemed a valuable supplement and ultimately a worthy successor to current U.S. doctrines, including AirLand Battle. How might such a doctrine come to fruition? What are some of the key challenges that would have to be faced?

We sense that the major challenges would be organizational. For example, if swarming is to work, jointness will have to broaden and deepen and be seriously regarded by all as a necessary condition for the rise of a doctrine that would seek to integrate both the data-gathering and the fire capabilities of all the services—in all sorts of settings, across the spectrum of intensity of future conflict.

Along with increased jointness, there will also have to be increased decentralization of the command and control of widely dispersed forces operating in a nonlinear battle-space. But there may be temptations to find new ways to exert more control from the top, since the new information and communications technologies can promise more timely central direction. Such temptations must be resisted. While "topsight" can have great value, using it for overcontrol from the top would court disaster in swarming operations.

Instead, those aspects of "network-centric warfare" and the "system of systems" that foster networking and decentralization should be vigorously developed. They offer the best chances to move from the generally hierarchical approach to war that currently characterizes U.S. military doctrine, toward an alternate paradigm in which hybrids of hierarchies and networks can flourish. The organizational choice is not a stark one between network and hierarchy; in between lies the possibility of a skillful blending of the two forms.

Another organizational point concerns the place of IO in the rise of swarming, and in the more general future of U.S. military doctrine. So far, IO has been viewed mainly as a way to strike an adversary's communications and other information flows. To be sure, this is a worthy task. But a broader concept of IO makes sense, entailing better management of one's own information capabilities and resources. Developing IO in this light may be essential for swarming, since its effectiveness will depend on achieving higher levels of information management than any military doctrine has ever achieved. IO is not simply a specialty function to be called upon to help out in a tight spot in countering an enemy. Instead, IO may well lie at the heart of the management methods that will be required to make swarming work. This view of the primacy of the managerial aspect of information operations suggests that IO is—or should be viewed as—an integral aspect of all military operations.

If networked information resource management is indeed an enabler of swarming, then it will be necessary to think through the requirements that may be imposed by coalition operations. Assuring timely flows of sensitive, combat-urgent intelligence and other information may require the sharing of some of the U.S. military's most proprietary technologies and processes. It may well be that some allies will want to be brought into the networks that make up BattleSwarm. But not all allies are "created equal." All should not expect access to the most sensitive information flows. In the Gulf War, for example, U.S. allies included both Britain and Syria, the latter a long-time sponsor of international terrorism, according to the U.S. State Department. How can a swarm's needs for full information sharing be reconciled with the constraints imposed by a coalition that may include semitrusted partners?

We raise this issue here in the hope that this concern will be addressed by future research. The answer to coalition IO questions will bear heavily upon the future of swarming. Coalitions have often functioned well when the partners have possessed quite different skill levels. In the Gulf War, for example, the "left hook" was undertaken principally by American and British forces, while far less demanding, but still important, tasks were assigned to the Syrians. Thus, it may be that future coalitions may feature many nonswarming operations by members engaging in holding or other less-advanced actions—which nevertheless support the movements of the swarming force.

Technological hurdles also loom large on the path to BattleSwarm. First, aside from the challenge of assuring the internetting of communications among myriad units, it is imperative that communications also be hardened and made redundant. An enemy who knows that information operations lie at the enabling core of swarming will surely strike at them—and we must prepare to parry such blows in advance. It may also be possible to safeguard a swarm force's information flows by means of decoys and deception. Indeed, the use of false or enhanced signals and traffic may prove to have offensive, in addition to defensive, utility.

There is also a technological dimension to the coalition question. It is the technical counterpart to the political concerns that attend the idea of sharing sensitive data with allies who are only semitrusted. Simply put, combined operations require robust communications interoperability among coalition partners. Yet, technically enabling a coalition swarm may engender prohibitively high information security risks. It may turn out that the best remedy is not a technical one. Perhaps, instead, U.S. forces could specialize in swarming (i.e., in "hitting"), while our coalition partners would focus on more traditional "holding" and other conventional maneuver operations. (This suggestion has a historical precedent in the military of the Byzantine Empire, whose mobile cavalry formed the core of its military. The imperial cavalry adopted swarming as their key fighting doctrine (Van Creveld, 1989, p. 21) but encouraged their allies to operate more traditionally—a case of military specialization that worked well (Oman, 1924).)

We conclude this study with the thought that the United States may well be in a period between major military challenges—as in earlier "interwar" periods, such as the time between the World Wars. As this seems the case, we would like to argue that this period should be seen as one in which we have a luxury of time—and an absence of serious threats to our survival—in which we should be able to make the shift from an industrial- to an information-age military doctrine. The problem with interwar periods, though, is that their principal benefit—time—tends to be offset by a lack of urgency to initiate major changes.

Perhaps we can nudge matters a bit by suggesting that this a is period of *urgent luxury.* That is, despite America's unparalleled power and preponderance in world affairs, the pace of the information revolution is so quick that, should we not innovate, adept adversaries could make serious inroads into our security in a short time. One need only look to the 1930s—when the panzer division and the Stuka dive bomber upset the balance of power in just a few short years—to know that "luxury," in military matters, is almost always fleeting.

BIBLIOGRAPHY

Addington, Larry H., *The Blitzkrieg Era and the German General Staff,* New Brunswick: Rutgers University Press, 1971.

Alexander, Bevin, *The Future of Warfare,* New York: W.W. Norton, 1995.

Arquilla, John, "The Strategic Implications of Information Dominance," *Strategic Review,* Vol. 22, No. 3, Summer 1994, pp. 21–27.

Arquilla, John, and Theodore Karasik, "Chechnya: A Glimpse of Future Conflict?" *Studies in Conflict and Terrorism,* Vol. 22, No. 3, July–September 1999, pp. 207–230.

Arquilla, John, and David Ronfeldt, "Cyberwar Is Coming," *Comparative Strategy,* Vol. 12, No. 2, Summer 1993, pp. 141–165.

Arquilla, John, and David Ronfeldt, *The Advent of Netwar,* Santa Monica: RAND, 1996.

Arquilla, John, and David Ronfeldt, eds., *In Athena's Camp: Preparing for Conflict in the Information Age,* Santa Monica: RAND, 1997.

Arquilla, John, and David Ronfeldt, "Preparing for Information-Age Conflict, Part I: Conceptual and Organizational Dimensions," *Information, Communication, and Society,* Vol. 1, No. 1, Spring 1998a, pp. 1–22.

Arquilla, John, and David Ronfeldt, "Preparing for Information-Age Conflict, Part II: Doctrinal and Strategic Dimensions," *Information, Communication, and Society,* Vol. 1, No. 2, Summer 1998b, pp. 121–143.

Arquilla, John, and David Ronfeldt, *The Emergence of Noopolitik: Toward an American Information Strategy,* Santa Monica: RAND, 1999.

Arquilla, John, David Ronfeldt, and Michele Zanini, "Information-Age Terrorism," *Current History,* Vol. 99, No. 636, April 2000, pp. 179–185.

Ashley, Percy, *Europe from Waterloo to Sarajevo*, New York: Knopf, 1926.

Barzun, Jacques, *Introduction to Naval History*, New York: Lippincott, 1944.

Bekker, Cajus, *The Luftwaffe War Diaries*, New York: Doubleday, 1967.

Benét, Stephen Vincent, *America*, New York: Farrar & Rinehart, 1944.

Benford, James, *High-Power Microwaves*, London: Artec, Inc., 1998.

Bennett, Geoffrey, *The Battle of Jutland*, London: Batsford, 1964.

Black, Jeremy, *European Warfare, 1660–1815*, New Haven: Yale University Press, 1994.

Blumenson, Martin, *The Duel for France, 1944*, Boston: Houghton Mifflin, 1963.

Bonabeau, Eric, Marco Dorigo, and Guy Theraulaz, *Swarm Intelligence: From Natural to Artificial Systems*, Oxford: Oxford University Press, 1999.

Bowden, Mark, *Blackhawk Down: A Story of Modern War*, New York: Atlantic Monthly Press, 1999.

Breuer, William B., *Hoodwinking Hitler: The Normandy Deception*, New York: Praeger, 1993.

Brodie, Bernard, *Sea Power in the Machine Age*, Princeton: Princeton University Press, 1943.

Bywater, Hector, *The Great Pacific War*, Boston: Houghton Mifflin (reprinted by St. Martin's Press, 1991), 1925.

Carell, Paul, *Invasion—They're Coming!* New York: E. P. Dutton, 1960.

Carell, Paul, *Scorched Earth: The Russian-German War, 1943–1944*, Boston: Little, Brown and Company, 1966.

Carlyle, Thomas, *The French Revolution: A History*, New York: Random House, [1837] 1955.

Carr, Edward Hallett, *Studies in Revolution*, London: Macmillan, 1950.

Cebrowski, Vice Admiral Arthur, and John Garstka, "Network-Centric Warfare," *Proceedings of the United States Naval Institute*, Vol. 124, No. 1, January 1998, pp. 28–35.

Chambers, James, *The Devil's Horsemen*, New York: Atheneum, 1985.

Chandler, David, *The Campaigns of Napoleon*, New York: Scribner, 1966.

Churchill, Winston, *Their Finest Hour,* Vol. 2 of *The Second World War,* Boston: Houghton Mifflin Company, 1949.

Clausewitz, Carl von, *On War,* Princeton: Princeton University Press, [1831] 1976.

Cleaver, Harry, "The Zapatistas and the Electronic Fabric of Struggle," 1995 (http://www.eco.utexas.edu/faculty/Cleaver/zaps.html). Print publication in John Holloway and Eloina Pelaez, eds., *Zapatista! Reinventing Revolution in Mexico,* Sterling, VA: Pluto Press, 1998a, pp. 81–103.

Cleaver, Harry, "The Zapatista Effect: The Internet and the Rise of an Alternative Political Fabric," *Journal of International Affairs,* Vol. 51, No. 2, Spring 1998b, pp. 621–640.

Collins, Larry, and Dominique LaPierre, *Freedom at Midnight,* New York: Simon & Schuster, 1975.

Cordesman, Anthony, and Abraham Wagner, *The Lessons of Modern War, Vol. III, The Afghan and Falklands Conflicts,* Boulder: Westview Press, 1990.

Coroalles, Anthony M., "The Master Weapon: The Tactical Thought of J.F.C. Fuller Applied to Future War," *Military Review,* Vol. 71, No. 1, January 1991, pp. 62–72.

Creasy, Edward S., *Fifteen Decisive Battles of the World,* London: J. Bentley, 1851.

Cummins, John, *Francis Drake,* New York: St. Martin's Press, 1995.

Curtin, Jeremiah, *The Mongols: A History,* Boston: Little, Brown and Company, 1908.

Danitz, Tiffany, and Warren P. Strobel, "The Internet's Impact on Activism: The Case of Burma," *Studies in Conflict and Terrorism,* Vol. 22, No. 3, July–September 1999, pp. 257–269.

Danitz, Tiffany, and Warren P. Strobel, *Networking Dissent: Cyber Activists Use the Internet to Promote Democracy in Burma,* Washington, D.C.: United States Institute of Peace, Virtual Diplomacy Series, No. 3, February 2000.

De Armond, Paul, *Netwar in the Emerald City,* Public Good Project, Bellingham, WA, February 2000a (http://www.nwcitizen.com/publicgood/reports/wto).

De Armond, Paul, "Black Flag over Seattle," *Albion Monitor,* (Sebastopol, CA), No. 72, February 29, 2000b (http://www.monitor.net/monitor/seattlewto/index.html).

De Chair, Somerset, ed., *Napoleon on Napoleon: An Autobiography of the Emperor,* London: Cassell, 1992.

Deighton, Len, *Fighter: The True Story of the Battle of Britain,* London: Jonathan Cape, 1977.

Delbrueck, Hans, *The Barbarian Invasions,* Vol. 2 of *History of the Art of War,* Lincoln: University of Nebraska Press, [1921] 1990.

DeSeversky, Alexander, *Victory Through Air Power,* New York: Simon and Schuster, 1942.

Doenitz, Karl, *Memoirs: Ten Years and Twenty Days,* Cleveland: World Publishing Co., 1959.

Douhet, Giulio, *The Command of the Air,* New York: McCann, 1942.

Dyer, Gwynne, *War,* New York: Crown Publishers, 1985.

Ederington, L. Benjamin, and Michael J. Mazarr, eds., *Turning Point: The Gulf War and U.S. Military Strategy,* Boulder: Westview Press, 1994.

Edwards, Sean J. A., "The Threat of High Altitude Electromagnetic Pulse to Force XXI," *National Security Studies Quarterly,* Autumn 1997, pp. 61–80.

Edwards, Sean J. A., *Swarming on the Battlefield: Past, Present, and Future,* Santa Monica, CA: RAND, 2000.

Ellis, John, *Brute Force: Allied Strategy and Tactics in the Second World War,* New York: Viking Press, 1990.

Evans, Howard E., ed., *Insect Biology,* Reading: Addison-Wesley, 1984.

Farris, William Wayne, *Heavenly Warriors: The Evolution of the Japanese Military, 500–1300,* East Asian Monograph No. 157, Cambridge: Harvard University Press, 1996.

Feifer, George, *Tennozan,* New York: Ticknor & Fields, 1992.

Ferrill, Arther, *The Origins of War: From the Stone Age to Alexander the Great,* London: Thames & Hudson, 1985.

Fischer, David Hackett, *Paul Revere's Ride,* New York: Oxford University Press, 1994.

Forrest, Stephanie, A. S. Perelson, L. Allen, and R. Cherukuri, "Self-Non-Self Discrimination in a Computer," *Proceedings of the IEEE Symposium: Research in Security and Privacy,* Washington, D.C., 1994.

Freedman, Lawrence, and Efraim Karsh, *The Gulf Conflict, 1990–1991,* Princeton: Princeton University Press, 1993.

Friedman, George, and Meredith Friedman, *The Future of War,* New York: Crown Publishers, 1996.

Friedman, Norman, *Desert Victory: The War for Kuwait,* Annapolis: Naval Institute Press, 1991.

Fuentes, Gidget, "Return to the Urban Jungle," *Marine Corps Times,* March 20, 2000.

Fuller, J.F.C., *The Generalship of Alexander the Great,* New Brunswick: Rutgers University Press, 1960.

Gall, Carlotta, and Thomas de Waal, *Chechnya: Calamity in the Caucasus,* New York: New York University Press, 1998.

Galland, Adolf, *The First and the Last,* London: Methuen, 1973.

Gann, Lewis, *Guerrillas in History,* Stanford: Hoover Institution Press, 1970.

Gelernter, David, *Mirror Worlds, or the Day Software Puts the Universe in a Shoebox . . . How It Will Happen and What It Will Mean,* New York: Oxford University Press, 1991.

Glasstone, Samuel, and Philip J. Dolan, *The Effects of Nuclear Weapons,* Washington, D.C.: U.S. Government Printing Office, 1977.

Gottfried, Kurt, and Bruce G. Blair, eds., *Crisis Stability and Nuclear War,* New York: Oxford University Press, 1988.

Gotwald, William, *Army Ants: The Biology of Social Predation,* Ithaca: Cornell University Press, 1995.

Graves, Robert, *Count Belisarius,* London: Cassells, 1938.

Griffith, Samuel B., *Mao Tse-Tung on Guerrilla Warfare,* New York: Praeger, 1961.

Guderian, Heinz, *Panzer Leader,* New York: Ballantine, 1957.

Hallion, David, *Storm Over Iraq: Air Power and the Gulf War,* Washington, D.C.: Smithsonian Institution Press, 1992.

Hastings, Max, *The Korean War,* New York: Simon & Schuster, 1987.

Hastings, Max, and Simon Jenkins, *The Battle for the Falklands,* New York: W. W. Norton, 1983.

Heilbrunn, Otto, *Conventional Warfare in the Nuclear Age,* London: George Allen and Unwin, Ltd., 1965.

Heyman, Charles, ed., *Jane's World Armies,* Alexandria, VA: Jane's Information Group, Inc., 1999.

Hölldobler, Bert, and Edward O. Wilson, *Journey to the Ants*, Cambridge: Harvard University Press, 1994.

Hough, Richard, *The Fleet That Had to Die*, New York: Viking Press, 1958.

Hoyt, Erich, *The Earth Dwellers: Adventures in the Land of Ants*, New York: Simon & Schuster, 1996.

Hughes, Wayne, "22 Questions for Streetfighter," *Naval Proceedings*, Vol. 126, No. 2, February 2000, pp. 46–49.

Hughes, Wayne, *Fleet Tactics*, Annapolis: Naval Institute Press, 1986.

Jomini, Antoine Henri de, *The Art of War*, London: Greenhill, [1838] 1992.

Jones, Reginald, *The Wizard War*, New York: Coward, McCann & Geoghegan, Inc., 1978.

Jordan, Brian, *The Athenian Navy in the Classical Period*, Berkeley: University of California Press, 1975.

Kahn, David, *Seizing the Enigma*, Boston: Houghton Mifflin, 1993.

Keegan, John, *The First World War*, London: Random House (Porter Books), 1998.

Keegan, John, *A History of Warfare*, New York: Random House, 1993.

Keegan, John, *The Second World War*, New York: Viking Press, 1989.

Kelly, Kevin, *Out of Control: The Rise of Neo-Biological Civilization*, New York: Addison-Wesley Publishing Company, 1994.

Kephart, J. O., "A Biological-Inspired Immune System for Computers," in R.A. Brooks and P. Maies, eds., *Artificial Life*, Cambridge: MIT Press, 1994.

Kobrin, Stephen J., "The MAI and the Clash of Globalizations," *Foreign Policy*, No. 112, Fall 1998, pp. 97–109.

Krepinevich, Andrew, *The Army and Vietnam*, Baltimore: Johns Hopkins University Press, 1986.

Lesser, Ian O., Bruce Hoffman, John Arquilla, David Ronfeldt, and Michele Zanini, *Countering the New Terrorism*, Santa Monica: RAND, 1999.

Libicki, Martin, *The Mesh and the Net: Speculations on Armed Conflict in a Time of Free Silicon*, Washington, D.C.: National Defense University Press, 1994.

Liddell Hart, B. H., *Great Captains Unveiled*, London: Jonathan Cape, 1927.

Liddell Hart, B. H., *The Real War, 1914–1918*, Boston: Little, Brown and Company, 1930.

Lieven, Anatol, *Chechnya: Tombstone of Russian Power,* New Haven: Yale University Press, 1998.

Lorenz, Konrad, *On Aggression,* New York: Harcourt Brace, 1966.

MacGregor, Douglas, *Breaking the Phalanx: A New Design for Landpower in the 21st Century,* New York: Praeger, 1997.

Macintyre, Donald, *The Naval War Against Hitler,* New York: Charles Scribner's Sons, 1971.

Maclear, Michael, *The Ten Thousand Day War: Vietnam, 1945–1975,* New York: St. Martin's Press, 1981.

Mahan, A. T., *The Influence of Sea Power upon History, 1660–1783,* Boston: Little, Brown and Company, 1890.

Mahan, A. T., *The Influence of Sea Power Upon the French Revolution and Empire, 1793–1812,* 2 vols., Boston: Little, Brown and Company, 1894.

Mahan, Alfred T., *The Life of Nelson,* 2 vols., Boston: Little, Brown and Company, 1898.

Marcus, G. J., *A Naval History of England: The Formative Centuries,* Boston: Little, Brown and Company, 1961.

Matsumura, John, Randall Steeb, Thomas Herbert, Scot Eisenhard, John Gordon, Mark Lees, and Gail Halverson, *The Army After Next: Exploring New Concepts and Technologies for the Light Battle Force,* Santa Monica: RAND, 1999.

McNeill, William H., *The Pursuit of Power,* Chicago: University of Chicago Press, 1982.

Mellenthin, Major General F. W. von, *Panzer Battles: A Study of the Employment of Armor in the Second World War,* Tulsa: University of Oklahoma Press, 1956.

Millett, Allan, and Peter Maslowski, *For the Common Defense: A Military History of the United States,* New York: Free Press, 1994 [revised and expanded edition].

Mitchell, William, *Memoirs of World War I,* New York: Random House, [1928] 1960.

Montgomery, Viscount Bernard L., *A History of Warfare,* Cleveland: World Publishing, 1968.

Morris, Donald R., *The Washing of the Spears: A History of the Rise of the Zulu Nation Under Shaka and Its Fall in the Zulu War of 1879,* New York: Simon & Schuster, 1965.

Oman, Charles, *A History of the Art of War in the Middle Ages,* London: Oxford University Press, 1924.

Overy, Richard, "Air Warfare," in Charles Townshend, *The Oxford Illustrated History of Modern War*, London: Oxford University Press, 1997.

Owens, William A., *High Seas: The Naval Passage to an Uncharted World*, Annapolis: Naval Institute Press, 1995.

Padfield, Peter, *Armada*, Annapolis: Naval Institute Press, 1988.

Page, Robert Morris, *The Origin of Radar*, New York: Doubleday, 1962.

Pape, Robert A., *Bombing to Win: Airpower and Coercion in War*, Ithaca: Cornell University Press, 1995.

Phillips, Lieutenant Colonel Edward L., "Special Forces Direct Action," *Special Warfare*, Vol. 8, No. 2, April 1995.

Phillips, T. R., ed., *The Roots of Strategy*, New York: Columbia University Press, 1943.

Prados, John, *Combined Fleet Decoded: The Secret History of American Intelligence and the Japanese Navy in World War II*, New York: Random House, 1995.

Roberts, Michael, "The Military Revolution, 1560–1660," from his *Essays in Swedish History*, London: Weidenfeld and Nicolson, 1967.

Rodgers, William Ledyard, *Greek and Roman Naval Warfare*, Annapolis: Naval Institute Press, 1937.

Rodgers, William Ledyard, *Naval Warfare Under Oars: 4th to 16th Centuries*, Annapolis: Naval Institute Press, 1940.

Ronfeldt, David, *Tribes, Institutions, Markets, Networks: A Framework About Societal Evolution*, Santa Monica: RAND, 1996.

Ronfeldt, David, John Arquilla, Graham Fuller, and Melissa Fuller, *The Zapatista 'Social Netwar' in Mexico*, Santa Monica: RAND, 1998.

Royko, Mike, *Boss: Richard J. Daley of Chicago*, New York: E. P. Dutton, 1971.

Rumpf, Hans, *The Bombing of Germany*, New York: Holt, Rinehart and Winston, 1962.

Russ, Martin, *Breakout: The Chosin Reservoir Campaign, Korea 1950*, New York: Fromm International, 1999.

Sansom, George, *History of Japan to 1334*, Stanford: Stanford University Press, 1958.

Schneirlea, Theodore, *Army Ants: A Study in Social Organization*, San Francisco: Freeman & Co., 1971.

Sélincourt, Aubrey de, *Arrian's the Campaigns of Alexander*, London: Penguin, 1958.

Skocpol, Theda, *States and Social Revolutions*, Cambridge: Cambridge University Press, 1979.

Sorley, Lewis, *A Better War*, New York: Harcourt Brace, 1999.

Spector, Ronald, *Eagle Against the Sun: The American War with Japan*, New York: The Free Press, 1985.

Starr, Chester G., *The Influence of Sea Power on Ancient History*, London: Oxford University Press, 1989.

Steeb, Randall, John Matsumura, Terrell Covington, Thomas Herbert, Scot Eisenhard, and Laura Melody, *Rapid Force Projection Technologies: A Quick-Look Analysis of Advanced Light Indirect Fire Systems*, Santa Monica: RAND, 1996.

Stone, I. F., *The Trial of Socrates*, New York: Doubleday, 1989.

Sullivan, John, "Third Generation Street Gangs: Turf, Cartels, and Net Warriors," *Transnational Organized Crime*, Vol. 3, No. 3, Autumn 1997, pp. 95–108.

Thomson, G. M., *Sir Francis Drake*, New York: Morrow, 1972.

Toffler, Alvin, and Heidi Toffler, *War and Anti-War: Survival at the Dawn of the Twenty First Century*, Boston: Little, Brown and Company, 1993.

Turney-High, H. H., *Primitive Warfare*, Columbia, SC: University of South Carolina Press, 1949.

Van Creveld, Martin, *Supplying War: Logistics from Wallenstein to Patton*, Cambridge: Cambridge University Press, 1977.

Van Creveld, Martin, *Technology and War*, New York: Free Press, 1989.

Van Creveld, Martin, *The Transformation of War*, New York: Free Press, 1991.

Warden, John A., *The Air Campaign*, Washington, D.C.: National Defense University Press, 1988.

Wedgwood, C. V., *The Thirty Years War*, London: Jonathan Cape, 1938.

Weigley, Russell, *The American Way of War*, New York: Macmillan, 1973.

Wellman, Paul I., *Indian Wars of the West*, New York: Marboro, 1992 edition.

Wilson, Edward O., *The Insect Societies*, Cambridge: Harvard University Press, 1971.

Winterbotham, F. W., *The Ultra Secret*, New York: Harper & Row, 1974.

Wood, Derek, and Derek Dempster, *The Narrow Margin: The Battle of Britain and the Rise of Air Power, 1930–1940*, London: Hutchinson, 1961.

Wootton, Anthony, *Insects of the World*, London: Blandford Press, 1984.

Wright, Robert, *Dowding and the Battle of Britain*, London: MacDonald, 1969.

Yamada, Nakaba, *Ghenko: The Mongol Invasion of Japan*, New York: Dutton, 1916.

Zanini, Michele, "Middle Eastern Terrorism and Netwar," *Studies in Conflict and Terrorism*, Vol. 22, No. 3, July–September 1999, pp. 247–256.

Zedong, Mao, *On Guerrilla Warfare*, Griffith translation, New York: Praeger, 1961.